WINNING
JERSEY STYLE

DON SOMMA

authorHOUSE®

AuthorHouse™
1663 Liberty Drive
Bloomington, IN 47403
www.authorhouse.com
Phone: 1-800-839-8640

Published by AuthorHouse   02/14/2012

ISBN: 978-1-4685-4236-3 (sc)
ISBN: 978-1-4685-4238-7 (hc)
ISBN: 978-1-4685-4237-0 (ebk)

Library of Congress Control Number: 2012900720

Acknowledgements

Many thanks to the following for their vital part in my story . . .

. . . my entire family for all of their love, support, and coaching.

. . . every young man and young woman that I was associated with as a teacher, coach, and friend.

. . . my fellow teachers, coaches, school administrators, parents, and support groups who worked along with me toward helping students grow in a positive way.

. . . my typist, Judy Barry, and my writing coach, Al Chaput.

. . . and Walter, our friend at Starbucks in Bluffton, SC.

And finally, my deepest thanks to my wife, Susan, and to our daughters, Gretchen and Heidi, for being my best friends and my loyal fans every step of the way. Without them this book would have been impossible, and it is to them that this book is dedicated.

"I'd rather calm down a crazy man,
than to try to wake the dead."

. . . Don Somma, 1971

ONE

My grandfather, Tony Ragnoni, was quite a man to learn from. He was a hard-working New Jersey boilermaker who walked six miles every day to and from work. Bound Brook was a town of approximately eight thousand residents and was a true melting pot made up of Italians, Polish, Black Americans and Irish. It was a great community with little or no prejudice. Everyone respected each other and interacted very well.

Grandpop put his hard fifty in every week. Come weekends it was all about family and making a few visits to the "Sons' of Italy" for some cold beer, good wine and great conversation with the other hard-working men of the neighborhood.

Those forty-eight hours he had during the weekend were very special to him. No time to waste. Between naps and sleeping, eighteen hours were spent. Ten hours were spent in the yard or his wine cellar. Working in the yard, his chores of choice were tending the garden, nurturing his grapes and taking care of the chickens as a food source.

In his wine cellar, he would make his wine and distill grappa, along with making a beautiful sausage. Also here you would find the greatest cheeses from my aunt's grocery store hanging in a symphony of flavors.

Continuing on my grandfather's clock—five hours were spent at the "Sons' of Italy." The final fifteen hours were spent doing what I truly believe he enjoyed best . . . eating, playing with his grandchildren and sitting on his front porch talking, smoking his stogies, and enjoying his beer and wine. My grandfather was definitely the boss of yard, wine cellar and front porch.

An incident occurred one day when I was five that really made an impression on me about being on time and acting upon a command.

Grandpop only had so much time to do this or that, and one of the things he had to do was feed the chickens. If it was a Saturday night and we were going to have fresh chicken on Sunday, one had to go. Which one? How did he choose?

He would call the chickens. He would say, "venire qui" which means 'come here' in Italian and they'd better come a-running. The longer it took, the more time wasted and he didn't like wasting time on someone or something not listening to him when he gave an order.

Well, the chickens would come. The last one there would be swept up with his big hands and in one motion the neck was broken and the head came off. He would throw the chicken on the ground, put the head on his finger and chase my cousin, Anthony, and me around with the head of the chicken hitting us lovingly on the noggin, while the chicken ran in circles bleeding to death. He would laugh and say, "See what happens when you don't listen and you're late."

Boy, what a learning experience for a five-year old. Talk about making a point. I still can visualize this man with his stogie in one hand and the chicken head on the other hand laughing and enjoying his own humor. This memory has stayed with me all my life and definitely was a life lesson learned at a young age.

*   *   *

Sports were very important in the neighborhood. You could usually find a pick-up game of some kind of baseball in the summer, football in the fall and basketball in the winter. If there wasn't a pick-up game, there were a lot of unique ways to work on the skills needed to play one of those three sports.

A good example of keeping myself occupied while improving a skill was my taking an old broomstick handle, finding a pile of stones, throwing one stone at a time up in the air and hitting it using the broom handle as a bat. It was a great way to improve bat speed by swinging a stick, and to improve my eye by taking this "skinny bat" and hitting the small stone. Repetition—repetition—always competing against self. See how many I could hit in a row, always trying to break my old record.

If you weren't playing sports in your free time you were usually talking about it. The love of professional sports, the Yankees, Dodgers and Giants in baseball; the Giants in football, the Knicks in basketball and the Rangers in hockey, was very evident in my family. As far back as I can remember, my father, his three brothers, and my grandpop on my father's side agreed on who they would support in basketball, football and hockey because there was only one local team for each professional sport except in baseball. Here was where the competitive attitude amongst these stubborn Italians would surface. I still remember the arguments—who was better, the "Duke," "Joe D" or the "Say Hey Kid?" Every one of them had their turn in the limelight.

The reality of it all was the hometown heroes were the ones who received the most notoriety. My grandpop managed a baseball team that my father and brother played on. Everyone on the team was related in one way or another. The games were family events. Win or lose, when it was over everyone interacted around a dish of Grandma's macaroni and a glass of homemade wine. My Uncle "Nick," my father's youngest brother, was special. As a junior in high school in 1942, he pole vaulted twelve feet with an iron pole. That record lasted for some time. But when he came home from World War II, he built his legend by being a fast pitch softball pitcher for hire. He was unbelievable!

Every organized fast pitch softball team wanted him to pitch for them. Local companies always tried to sway him to play for them by offering him a job or other financial perks. He would take me along with him to games when I was old enough. I observed the competitive atmosphere of those fast pitch games when I was ten. To the victor went the spoils. The night my uncle pitched against the famous King and His Court and beat them, the celebration and rewards went on for days. Uncle Nick was my number one sports idol.

During my formative years, I wanted to be a part of this local sports notoriety and town pride. Bound Brook High School was a few blocks from my house. As I got older and was given more freedom to roam on my own, I found my way to the high school practice field.

During the fall, I really enjoyed spending my playtime there. Before long, I was utilizing the seven man sled when it wasn't being used by the team. I would work on perfecting my "flipper."

The forearm was quite a weapon, if used properly. It was a way to destroy your opponent's attempt to make a block on you. This single maneuver was the foundation of being a good defender. You had to get off the block to enable yourself to get in a good position to make the tackle. I worked on it every day and after practice sometimes I would get personal attention from either a coach or a player who would spare a few minutes before dashing off to the locker room.

Before long, I was helping the players clean up after practice, or running around getting things for the coaches. I belonged. I was part of the excitement. I was contributing to the team, and what a team they were. Our reward for all of the hard work was game time on Saturday afternoon.

From the pregame preparation to the parade back to the high school after a victory, Saturday was the highlight of the week. What a memorable experience. The football game and all its excitement was the focal point of this small town's entertainment and had people looking forward to Saturdays.

Football brought the community together for a Saturday afternoon. I mean everyone would be there. It was the thing to do, the place to be. After the excitement of the day, it would provide the conversation and bragging rights until the next game. Forget about who was better—the Giants or Dodgers. I was a member, a contributing member to the high school football team and my sports idol wasn't the Duke or the Say Hey Kid. My idols were now the players on the local teams, the people I could see and touch.

*   *   *

The "last great generation," a title given to my father's generation, was a special breed. One of the things I observed about the men I knew from that group was that almost all of them were not nine to five guys regarding how they supported their families. Almost all of them had their full-time jobs—but along with that they always had part-time jobs so they could support their families financially, and by doing this, their wives could stay home and run the house.

My father was no different. He was the head electrician at the county's water company where his normal work week was forty hours a week plus overtime. His side jobs were working at my Uncle's pizzeria and doing part-time electrical work for the textile mill in town. Along with this, he was selling Christmas trees and Easter flowers in season. He sure kept busy. In a normal work week he would labor between sixty-five to seventy-five hours. Mix all that in with always spending time with the family for suppers and his personal time was extremely limited.

When I was eleven, my father joined a family oriented golf club out in the country about a half hour from where we lived. He and his three brothers would find time to play a round or two of golf each week. This was his escape time. Not only did he enjoy it, he deserved a little free time from his many responsibilities.

On weekends in the summer my father would have my mother bring our family to the pool to meet him so we could, as a family, spend time together. My mother would pack an "Italian Picnic Basket." This basket would be filled with olives, peppers and various cheeses and salamis—a beautiful antipasto.

Along with this, there would be my mother's famous meatball and sausage sandwiches. My favorite was my mother's tomato salad, made from local New Jersey tomatoes, olive oil and fresh basil. It was great. To this day I can close my eyes and my taste buds still salivate over the thought of how delicious it was.

While waiting for my father to come, we would enjoy the pool with anticipation of how good our picnic was going to be. All the while we were in the pool we would look forward to his arrival.

For lunch the other families would go to either the pool snack bar which served hamburgers, hot dogs, French fries and local corn on the cob, or go inside the fancy clubhouse and have a sit down lunch or dinner. Not us. We would enjoy the pool and use the picnic area for our feast.

I often felt sorry for the other kids who had to eat the fast food at the pool or had to get dressed up and eat the fancy food that they served inside the clubhouse.

One Saturday afternoon, I spotted this beautiful girl splashing and swimming at the other end of the pool. I just had to go over to that end of the pool and get her attention. At eleven, I really didn't know how to do it, or if I should do it. I gave it some thought and came up with a plan. I figured I would do my famous "cannonball routine" which included about four different ways to disrupt the area with giant waves and splashes. Finally she noticed when I caused a major "splash" right next to her that got her hair wet. After many attempts I was successful. Did she notice me? Did she enjoy my routine? Did she want to be my new friend? Yes. She started walking toward me.

For the first and only time in my life, my heart skipped a beat, a beat that no other person could or would cause. I was so excited. Here she came. I was ready to say hello and tell her my name. She never stopped walking. She didn't even acknowledge me. This beautiful brown-eyed beauty walked right by me and directly toward my mother.

Now another new emotion, rejection. She went to my mother and asked her to please tell me to stop bothering her. Wow! Within five minutes three major emotions—love, rejection, and correction. Yes, my mother immediately corrected my behavior in a way only my mother could do. She made me sit out of the pool for the next half hour. During that half hour I made up my mind that somehow I wanted to become the girl's boyfriend.

Well, talk about being persistent. It took me seven years to finally get a date. All along I knew that someday I would ask her to be my wife. After two plus years of dating her and asking her twice to marry me, she finally said, "Yes" and we've been married now for forty-three years and counting. And yes, now she makes the "sauce" and boy can she make a good one.

I really believe if she would have tasted my mother's meatball sandwiches that first day she would have chosen to eat lunch with us instead of that country club food she and her family had to eat. And if that had happened, we definitely would have dated earlier instead of seven plus years down the road.

*　　*　　*

Growing up is learning the ability to deal with various situations that we are confronted with such as making friends, dealing with success or failure and just learning to communicate with your peers. These learning situations help us develop our personalities and hopefully add to our maturity. In junior high school, one of these hurdles I had to jump over was dealing with a bully.

As a young adolescent, rolling around and wrestling with my buddies was just a part of a normal day, plus I really enjoyed it. At least once a day, I would "play fight" either walking to school, on the playground or on my way home after a long school day. It was like two bear cubs rolling around in the woods.

"Play fighting" was just something you did. Your goal was not to hurt your buddy, just make him say "Uncle." As soon as that happened, you would be on to the next thing with no hard feelings, but you would already start scheming on how you would handle the next match. The problem with my school work was I never took it seriously. The only things I took seriously were playing around and physical education class. As you moved up to fifth grade there were extra-curricular athletics. My father was getting tired of my lack of classroom effort. Sooner or later it definitely was going to change one way or another.

In the seventh and eighth grade I was confronted with a person who just enjoyed taking advantage of his peers. He would somehow find a person's weakness and completely exploit this achilles heel.

My mother, grandmother and most female members of my family, along with the nuns at Catholic school, would always make the point that fighting, real fighting, was wrong. We should control our anger and do our best to turn the other cheek, love thy neighbor, and find a way to get along.

My method of getting along with this kid, who thought he was a "tough guy," was to be nice to him and allow him to be what he truly was, a bully. I never would confront his attitude. He smelled out my weakness. He knew I never wanted to have a real fight because I was taught it was wrong and a "good friend" didn't want to hurt his buddies. He recognized my kindness as a weakness and this bothered me.

After a year plus, and at times allowing this person to take advantage of my kindness, the opportunity finally presented itself to set the rules of our relationship straight.

It was a Saturday on a beautiful New Jersey fall morning and we had a sandlot football game planned. These sandlot games were great, everything about them was fun.

First you had to organize the playing field. This special morning we were going to have our game at the middle school. The sidelines were defined by the school building itself and on the other side a row of beautiful fall-colored maple trees. The goal lines were the door of the school entrance down to the door to the side entrance, a beautiful forty-yard by seventy-yard grand field. Every set of ten windows was a first down, so our "field of dreams" was just about as perfect a setting as you would want.

The next thing we had to do was pick the teams. Just about the same time we were going to choose up, out of the blue Mr. Tough Guy showed up. This was a first. He never before wanted to play football with us. The games were rough and tough, which was expected and accepted. We never wanted to hurt anyone, but the rougher the better.

He put out his cigarette and said he wanted to join us this memorable Saturday morning. And, he pushed his way into being one of the captains. After his first pick, it was time for the other captain to make his pick. My heart was racing. I so wanted to be on the other team. My wish came true. I was his opponent.

For the first time, I was really feeling anger simmering inside me. Finally, I was going to get a chance to be rough with him as my new found aggressiveness grew. Rage built, but because of my upbringing, I knew I had to control it, and control it I did.

My chance came early on in the game. It was their ball and Mr. Tough Guy was doing his best to control the game by telling everybody what to do in his bullying manner. He called a sweep toward the school building sidelines. I got him in my sights. I took an angle toward the point of impact, forcing him to decide to run into the building or cut back into my pursuit. So here he came right at me standing straight up, a beautiful target. In this one moment, I was about to end a year and a half of frustration of tolerating his attitude toward me, something I really disliked and which was embarrassing at times.

The moment played out in slow motion. I lined him up, dropped my hips and put myself in an explosive position. Just at the right time, I snapped and hit him not only enjoying the impact, but for a split second releasing a lot of frustration and anger, all perfectly timed like hooking a fish. I completed the perfect tackle. The kind when no one gets hurt, but the person knows he was hit. I mean, I really snapped into him; for a few seconds the world stopped. I was sure he was going to get up and want to fight.

He got up slowly knowing it was a clean hit, one that he initiated by cutting back toward me. It was either go out of bounds or face me. He chose me and at that point of impact respect, physical and emotional respect, was won. Finally I was off his list. That fast.

My first response was, wow! What a great game football was. You could win respect not just from your teammates, but also from your opponents for playing hard and rough the way the game was meant to be played within the lines with controlled rage, but always by the rules, never wanting to hurt but always letting the opponent know that at the moment of impact a point must be made.

*   *   *

The last week of eighth grade, the football coach came and held a meeting for all those interested in playing football in high school the coming fall. I was never so excited about attending a meeting. The day finally came. I ran to the meeting, went to the front row and sat on the edge of my seat, listening to every word the coach said—finally organized football. I couldn't wait to get home and tell my father all about it and get him to sign the permission slip.

My parents said when I got my last report card they would decide if they would sign the permission slip based on my progress. The next week I was on my best behavior at school, attempting to convince my teachers that I was trying my best. Well, my best wasn't good enough, another poor report card. My parents were really upset, especially my father.

In situations like this, my father was in charge of what decisions were going to be made. His decision was simple. He sat me down and said he wanted me to understand how it felt to not be allowed to do something I really wanted to do. He called the football coach and said he would not decide if I could play football in the fall until it was time to start practice. Also, he told me I wasn't allowed to play summer baseball.

Talk about being devastated. I was in a state of shock. I promised him I had learned my lesson. He said no promises. I had the summer to prove to him that my behavior and attitude towards school would have to change. He emphasized the point that I had to be more serious about learning and not just going to school because of play period, lunch and after school sports and playground.

The summer dragged by. My escape was that I worked at the local greenhouse with one of my friends during the day. At night, I went to the ball field and watched all my friends play ball. It about killed me. I was a spectator. Boy did I hate it. I had to be home each night before the street lights went on. I learned my lesson and promised myself this would never happen again.

The day before the first fall football meeting, my father still didn't let me know of his decision.

Finally, he sat me down and laid out the rules. He would allow me to play, but each week I would have to bring home a progress report and if my grades weren't at least a B average I wouldn't be allowed to play. It was a blessing in disguise. My father found my button. I never ever wanted to feel the way I did all summer—not being allowed to do something I loved because I was just lazy about school work.

The time finally came. It was time to take the challenge of paying attention in school and competing against myself to get good grades. I agreed to the rules and treated it like a game—me against the teacher, me against the subject matter. I knew I could do it because if I didn't, I knew my father wouldn't bend. He would bench me in a heartbeat. I knew once he made the rules of the game, he wouldn't bend them. So I treated it as a game, a game that I finally learned how to play because there was no choice. I had to win. Reality set in.

TWO

Right from the start, high school football sure opened my eyes wide as I had dreamed it would.

I loved everything about it from getting my equipment to my first full speed tackle. Because of my experience playing sandlot football with the older guys in town, I had already sized up the competition and believed I would make the varsity as a freshman. There were a couple of older guys in the neighborhood who drove. I knew if I played varsity I would work my way into their back seat and my problem of getting to and home from school would be solved—no longer hitching for a ride.

I loved the potential rewards of playing rough but fair. It was fair to block someone to the ground. It was fair to tackle someone and knock them to the ground. It was fair to have controlled rage and be aggressive. I pulled on everything I learned about the game hanging around those Bound Brook High School practices, those techniques that I spent hours on by myself to perfect. Now it was time, time to be a high school football player, time to make the varsity.

I was confident I was ready to play with the top players who were trying out for the varsity positions. I'd had my eye on the center and linebacker position for a long time going all the way back to how I got picked to play my first sandlot games.

I worked hard to be noticed that first day of "full contact," a chance to be judged on effort and to beat the man I lined up on, and then getting the chance to make the tackle as a reward.

It was a different era of football then. Certain rough techniques were allowed. Using the forearm shiver as an aggressive weapon was my favorite. Head tackling was legal so the game understandably was kind of extra rough. I still can hear, "Way to put your head in there." "Stick with your face."

Right from the start of the season I was playing varsity football for Middlesex High. It was great. Before we were halfway through the season, I was starting. I earned my position. What a good feeling. We did okay for a first year program. We took more beatings than we handed out but we got better at the end and we were gaining respect from our competitors.

Reward, especially earned reward, sure helped my confidence. My worries about getting to school and home from practice were solved. The guys in the neighborhood were letting me catch a ride. There sure were some neat cars then. Two older guys had classics, a forty-nine black Mercury, and a fifty-four Mercury with a sun roof.

There was enough "Real American Steel" in those two cars to keep a man working for a week in Detroit. Real leather seats and door panels, real leather rolled and pleated. There was enough room in the back seats to stretch out. I mean if you sat back against the rear seat your feet didn't reach the front seat. Relax, sit back, and enjoy the ride home listening to the local Motown station, WNJR. Boy, I really thought who "I" was.

Being known as a football player was "cool." Your teammates respected you and so did most of your classmates. Being classified as a "jock" wasn't sometimes as cool.

Well, in order to stay a part of this I had to keep the bargain I had with my parents about my good grades. Only B's or better were accepted.

More importantly I knew my father wouldn't bend. God bless him. Once he said, "That's it" he meant "That's it." No counting to three with him. No way. It actually became the norm and I stayed on the honor roll throughout high school. I finally looked forward to bringing my report card home and seeing how much joy it brought to my parents.

A whole new experience was taking place. I was leaving my secure neighborhood and venturing to other towns. Your reputation as a football player grew based on performance both individually and team-wise.

In Somerset and Middlesex Counties there was an abundance of small towns which bordered each other all within a twenty-mile radius. There were enough towns to fill a full football schedule and you never had to be on a bus for more than a half hour getting to any opponent's home field. My territory was growing.

Communication, the passing on of a message, reading your name in the paper was new and exciting. But, you knew your opponents were reading it also. For me it was exciting and finally rivalries were being built both individually and as a team.

Being recognized was personified by wearing a varsity jacket, especially wearing one as a freshman. You would definitely wear this "Coat of Arms" when you visited other towns. You were making a statement. I am from Middlesex and I do play football or baseball or whatever.

I was definitely building a memory bank. Over the next two years, we got better and started winning more games than we lost. The publicity got better, and by my junior year I began getting college interest letters.

I started to realize maybe I wanted to stay involved with this sport. Maybe I might want to go to college. Because of my father's rule about grades, I actually started enjoying the learning process. School was exciting and I definitely was enjoying everything about it.

I knew how hard my father and mother worked and saved to send my brother to college. Down deep inside that thought was that maybe I won't go to school. I'd open my business full time right out of high school and be my own man from the start. But as scholarship offers started to be talked about, and I would get a full football scholarship if I continued to improve, my thoughts were definitely changing. Yes, maybe I would become a physical education teacher and coach, plus there always were summers to have my own business and do odd jobs. Maybe I would follow the same path as my favorite high school coach. Teach, coach and run my own business.

*   *   *

Those high school years were quite a learning experience. Thank God you only got one chance to do it right.

There were certain groups of kids who got along with each other and socially hung out together. These groups were based upon what section of town you were from, what extracurricular activities you were involved with, how you chose to dress, were you a "greaser" or did you choose to dress in an "Ivy League style," etc. Right from the start I didn't like being categorized with any certain cliques. I liked both dressing with starched high roll shirts with my initial on the collar or wearing a Madras shirt and penny loafers.

My ability to get along with all different groups led to my political career on the high school level. I loved the concept of team and teamwork. I enjoyed watching things getting done. Goal setting and follow through was an exciting concept to be a part of.

With a little coaxing from various peer groups, I got involved with school government, being voted in as junior and senior class president. I definitely utilized my learned talents of getting people involved and accomplishing a common goal through hard work and self discipline. Learning that you must respect to be respected when dealing with your peers was something that I continually tried to do and at times I did it better than others.

There were some very strong personalities in our class of two hundred students. Everyone, or almost everyone, was definitely categorized. I tried my best to be a little of everything or at least get involved with all of the groups. I didn't have to excel in something to be a part of something. It was neat to have a very, very small part in the class play and it was just as sharp to be the captain of the football team. I guess I was learning about that important biblical phrase about "the first being last and the last being first." You didn't always have to be the star.

*   *   *

The football season was almost over and I was contacted by most of the colleges in the northeast about potential visits and scholarship offers. It was really exciting. They were checking me out in person or on film and I was doing the same. It was like being part of the TV game show, "The Dating Game." We were both investigating the opportunity.

One of my coaches, Coach Roma, was a Little All-American at Wofford College in Spartanburg, South Carolina. He said, after the head coach there watched film on me, he wanted me to visit the school and we would talk about a possible football scholarship offer.

I agreed with my coach and decided we would take a visit. It was the weekend before Thanksgiving, an off week in Jersey football. No game. The final game of the regular season was "Turkey Day."

My head coach let me miss Friday and Saturday practice so we could make the trip and be back for school and practice on Monday.

Coach Roma and I drove all night and arrived Friday morning. My Friday was spent resting, visiting the admissions office and checking the campus out. We had a great steak cook-out at the coach's house with a few players. Little did I realize how I was being sized up by all involved.

As the evening was winding down I was told that practice was at ten a.m. Get a good night's sleep. Be at the locker room at nine a.m. to check out equipment.

Equipment—practice—what was going on? This was a first. I must have visited fifteen schools to this point, never a practice. Coach Roma explained to me that the head coach wanted to offer me a full scholarship, but he really wanted to see me in action against my competition first.

Before I knew it I was lined up, ready for an Oklahoma Drill. Oklahoma Drill is one-on-one competition with a blocker. Once you shed the block, when you're the defender, you get the chance to make a tackle, a one-on-one tackle, and the basics of defensive football. You learn a lot about a person over a live fifteen second or less audition. I just didn't go once. I must have had half a dozen opportunities. Little did the head coach know that this drill was my favorite. Along with all the years of practicing the techniques needed, I came with an attitude. My attitude was this is all I have to do to get a full scholarship, win my one-on-ones.

I did good enough that as soon as practice was over the head coach called me into his office and offered me a full scholarship. A scholarship that I earned. Even though I didn't accept the Wofford offer, it always has meant a lot to me because of what I had to do that day to truly earn it, just win my one-on-ones. No other school made me scrimmage against possibly my new teammates.

*   *   *

After the season, scholarship opportunities were available and I visited most all of the northeast schools along with Notre Dame which offered me the opportunity to prep a year.

After visiting South Carolina, I was very impressed with both the school and its football program. The day I visited it was snowing when I left Jersey. When we landed in South Carolina three hours later, it was seventy degrees. I had a great visit, made a lot of good friends early on and after meeting Coach Bass and Coach Floyd I was very excited about the possibility of going there and becoming a Gamecock football player.

A week after my visit, Coach Bass and Coach Floyd came to my house for a home visit. This visit turned into a party. A couple of my uncles along with my grandpop came to the meeting. My mother made the typical four-course Sunday meal with homemade wine being served with every course along with flavored grappa for dessert. Boy, could they eat. After about three hours of eating and drinking, my father who didn't demand I do too many things said, "Don, I would like you to go to South Carolina." It was over—decision made.

Yes, I decided I really was going to go to college. All my expenses were going to be paid for—a full scholarship. My parents did not have to pay anything and there were ways to get spending money. You got a check each month for laundry. There was meal money after games and rewards from fans, so the burden of financial responsibility for me obtaining a college education was off of my parents and onto me. I felt great about it. I was contributing. It felt good to see how proud my parents were of my achievement.

The winter months went fast. I was working out at the gym real hard and earning money every way I could, from being a mason laborer to selling masonry repairs to working at my high school baseball coach's hardware store.

I really enjoyed working for my high school baseball coach. He was a fair guy. He would help anyone who needed a little side money. There was always something going on, from unloading trailers or boxcars to working around the yard, learning how to work with your hands, painting, landscaping, roofing, fixing, doing anything and everything. Plus, I was watching and learning how to be a businessman, from observing a man who was one of the best businessmen I ever was around. He sure knew how to solve problems, and get paid for it.

My life was full. I was riding a wave. It was now baseball season. I was a three-year varsity starter. I had been the varsity starting catcher since my freshman year and this year was going to be no different. We had a very good team returning.

Well, success is something you have to learn to deal with. I thought who I was. All my opponents knew me. I couldn't wait to compete again. Things started out too good. I hit a couple of homeruns in our scrimmages and then I hit a "blast" in our season home opener. I bought a Mickey Mantle thin handle thirty-five inch bat, heavy with a big head. I was swinging for the fences.

The next three games, I went one for ten swinging for those fences. Coach said before the fifth game that he was going to give the number two catcher the start. Boy, did he take advantage of the opportunity. Once he got into the lineup he was on a tear.

It was hard to swallow, but I was relegated to platoon playing and pinch hitting. But I learned from a good coach about performance and taking advantage of an opportunity to perform fair and square.

I learned to live with my challenge. I did my best at keeping score and being a part-time player, knowing the coach wasn't playing favorites. He was just playing the one who was performing the best. Everyone had their role. Mine was being a part-time player and when I wasn't, the scorebook was mine. Keeping score made me feel I was still contributing even though I was delegated to a part-time player for the first time in my high school baseball career.

THREE

The initial shock of being a college freshman in 1964 became a reality the first night in my University of South Carolina dorm room. No midnight snack of cold meatballs and a glass of milk with a big chunk of my mother's homemade egg bread to clean up the gravy. To add to the pain, I realized after my third day that my clothes didn't wash themselves. It was up to me to wash them or get them cleaned. Thank God there was a laundromat across from our dorm that did a great job. In those days as part of our scholarship they gave you laundry money. It was more than enough to keep you in clean underwear, sheets and clothes. Add these domestic problems to being a football player who was trying to make the team and a freshman trying to stay eligible getting passing grades. It was a real wake-up call.

Academically, I figured it out early. First, you had to go to class. Once that was accomplished, you had to sit in the front row, take good notes and make sure the professor knew your name. I also had to make it apparent to the teacher that I wanted to be taught and that it was important to me to learn. This simple plan kept me out of the athletic mandatory study hall and always on time to get my diploma. Getting a diploma in the sixties was really an accomplishment since probably less than twenty-five percent of major college football players did so.

Becoming a starter who was accepted by his teammates was a lot more difficult. I distinctly remember the first day of practice. I was on the third string. We had six plus teams. I didn't feel too bad. There were just two players ahead of me on the depth chart. Everyone was some kind of all-star or they wouldn't have been there. So you could imagine what those guys felt like who were on the last team or alternates for the last team. The coaches emphasized the point that it didn't matter where you were on the depth chart in the beginning, but where you were the week of our first game which was four weeks away.

Football is a type of game where it is kind of hard for a coach to play favorites. Maybe a favorite son or a local hero was given a little partiality early on, but once the "live hitting" started it didn't take long for the pecking order to be developed and respect was won.

One of my freshman coaches, who was a two-time All-Atlantic Coast Conference performer, was a graduate assistant working on his law degree. He realized I was a little homesick and upset that I wasn't on the first team yet. He said, "Stop worrying. Stay eligible. Go to class and give your personal best every practice, every drill and you will get noticed. And if you like, you can use my office phone to call home anytime you want." I don't know if he realized that that advice and offer kept me from packing my bags and going home. Thank you, Jim Moss.

Finally by the first freshman game I won a starting position and was game captain. Both of these rewards were something that the coaches decided. Acceptance from teammates came a little slower. Most all the players on the team were from South Carolina and Georgia, with maybe a half-dozen from other southern states. The northern boys, or as some called Yankees, stuck together. It was a slow process, but respect and acceptance came.

I told my father about the Yankee stuff. My dad told my brother who was extremely well read. He had a great answer for those comments about being from the north. He said to tell them my family migrated from southern Italy. He also told me about a famous Italian General named Mario Garibaldi who fought for the Confederacy. He jokingly said I should tell them I was related to him. How many of these southern boys had a Confederate General in their family tree? So between working my way up the depth chart, staying eligible and winning over the southern boys with my family heritage and competitiveness, things were on the upswing.

*   *   *

Freshman football season was over. But my personal football season wasn't. I was a lucky one. Coach Bass kept about seven of us off that freshman team to practice with the varsity for the final three weeks of the 1964 varsity season. We worked with the "Bo Hunks" which was the team comprised of players who weren't playing on Saturday. I was on the "Hunk" defensive scout team. I loved it. It definitely was a special fraternity, both athletically and socially. It was our job to get the varsity offense ready for game day.

During the last month of practice, by giving my best every day and enjoying it, I was gaining respect from the older guys and coaches, but more importantly, I was checking out my competition and realizing how hard I was going to have to work preparing for spring practice.

In the sixties, there was no restriction on what you could do regarding football practices in or out of season. Weight training wasn't a big thing yet. Three days a week we trained almost like boxers or combatants. Old school stuff was the method—chin-ups, dips, jump rope, push-ups, medicine ball. Exercises, exercises, and more exercises.

We spent about two hours with the last half hour being combatives, different kinds of wrestling, mostly ways to see who was both physically, and mentally tougher man-on-man.

I knew if I was going to make the varsity as a sophomore and not be red-shirted, which meant being held out of varsity competition so I would not use up a year of eligibility, I had to get stronger.

The football team didn't have any type of weight equipment. The place to work out with weights was the Columbia YMCA. It definitely was "hard core." How much could you bench, squat, or hang clean was more important than your grade point ratio.

The attendees to this man cave 1960's style were mostly comprised of a special breed who for whatever reason wanted to improve their status by their neck size or like myself realized how important this new form of training was.

It was now spring practice which was football practice for two months, about twice what they do now.

Scholarships were unlimited. There were probably just under two hundred players involved. Talk about competition and hitting. The coaches on the defensive side of the ball were fun to be around. Bud Carson, who later on in his career was a well known NFL coach, was our defensive coordinator, and another good coach, Dick Bestwick, was our linebacker coach. These guys were all business with real defensive personalities. Spring practice was fun and I enjoyed every snap, every rep, just everything about it. By the end of spring, I was on the varsity depth chart and had a good chance to make the team come fall.

Summer went fast between working as a union laborer throwing cement blocks around and working a jackhammer. I was getting into good shape but also making big money. Five dollars an hour was huge in 1965, minimum wage was a dollar twenty-five an hour, plus I felt like I was getting paid to train. I loved the hard work and the atmosphere around the jobsite.

The stories I heard and the things I learned were priceless. I was getting quite a different education than I was receiving in college. It was definitely teamwork, but a blue collar style. At night three times a week, I would make my way to a gym that was in Plainfield, New Jersey. It was exactly how you would picture one of the first weight rooms. Not like today. There were no women in the place. It was just hard core lifters doing something that they loved. Again status was gained by your neck size, not your IQ. But it served the purpose for me—get bigger and stronger.

By the time the summer was over and I was going back to South Carolina for my first year of varsity football, I had some important stats. I was benching over 300 pounds and my neck size was nineteen inches. Forget about reading books and trying to improve your academics over vacation. It was time to make the team along with earning some spending money.

*   *   *

1965 was going to be a positive year. Everyone loved the coaching staff. We were surrounded by hard workers and good coaches. The Gamecocks had a nice mixture of young players and veterans. Things looked promising for South Carolina football.

I was told before the first game that I was on the travel team. About a dozen or so of my freshman teammates were going to be on the varsity team. "Stay healthy, stay eligible, practice hard and you'll get playing time." Those words of advice by Coach Moss always stayed with me.

Early in the season, I was getting limited reps. I sure wanted to be on the field more. As the season progressed so did my playing time. It was exciting playing teams you had only read about—Georgia, Tennessee, Maryland and, yes, Alabama with its legendary coach, Bear Bryant.

I had my first varsity start at Virginia and got a piece of a punt block with Senior Stan Juk. It was some emotional moment.

Our season ended with a big win over Clemson. We also tied for the 1965 ACC Championship.

One of my fondest memories that year on a personal note was that I shook Bear Bryant's hand. As we came out of our locker room, there was the Bear checking us out. I just had to stop by and say, "Hello." I can still close my eyes and there he was with the cigarette dangling.

School was good. I was learning how to study and more importantly I had a good "game plan" on what it took to pass and stay out of the mandatory study hall. We had a super staff in place who loved coaching us. We had a lot of returning players who wanted to play for that group of coaches. So things were really on the upswing. This was going to be the year we were going to win the Atlantic Coast Conference outright and get to a Bowl.

The pilgrimages to the "Y" increased. We were even using weight training stations in our team pre-spring practice work-outs. But if you really believed and wanted the strength edge while working your way up the status ladder based on strength and the size of your neck, the dungeon weight room at the YMCA was the place you'd better find time for.

There were two benches in the room, the little bench in the corner with plastic weights for people who could not handle 250 pounds or better and, if you could bench 300 pounds plus, you got to work out on the good bench. Talk about feeling you'd really accomplished something, working out on the "good one," the red bench, made you feel special and I was enjoying that feeling by spring practice.

Spring practice was here and there were things you had to do each and every day. I had to wake up, straighten my room, go to breakfast, make sure I was never late or missed class. I followed my plan on how to stay eligible plus again I was enjoying learning. Being a physical education major with a minor in Art, classes were fun and I was learning about things that I liked.

After classes I would have lunch, then get ready for practice or my journey to the "Y". Our training rules for what we could do with our free time were simple. "Don't get in trouble. Don't embarrass yourself or your school." If you did, your position coach would handle it. If it was something that was embarrassing to the program you went to Coach Bass's office and he would discipline you fair and square. The little free time I had, I enjoyed having a beer or two at some places within walking distance of campus or going to the movies with some real movie critic teammates.

My highlight of those days was when it was time to go to practice. Practice was my focal point. I was learning that desire overcomes ability.

Spring was going good. I was on the first team playing Middle Guard. My position coach was Ralph Floyd, the coach who recruited me who later on in his career became the athletic director at Indiana. Our team was looking sharp, and I was enjoying everything about practice. The greater the challenge, the more I enjoyed it.

All of a sudden the earth stopped spinning. Spring practice was about one-third complete. When the morning paper read "Coach Bass Steps Down as Head Coach of the Gamecocks," there wasn't a dry eye among the football family and team that day. He was a beloved man and coach. The reasons for him stepping down and becoming the head football coach in the Canadian Football League were never clear. Bottom line, he was no longer our coach.

Coach Bass was a real player's coach on and off the field. He was strict, but fair, his door was always open and if you ever got in trouble he was there. And then if you needed discipline you got a fair dose. Then he forgave you.

Coach Floyd became our interim head coach and all the players hoped he would get the job, especially the defensive line guys.

With about one third of spring practice left, new headlines—"South Carolina Hires Paul Dietzel to be the Head Football Coach." Coach Dietzel's resume had some impressive teams, one of those being a national championship team at Louisiana State University in 1958. For the last five or six seasons he was at West Point.

Vietnam became a big thing during that era and he was having a tough time recruiting. He was under pressure on the Hudson River, so the South Carolina opportunity was interesting and he took the job. In comes a new coach along with a new staff. This staff made it clear right from the start that a lot of us wouldn't make it through the initial evaluation practice. It was like they wanted to run off the players that were there and bring in their own boys.

All of a sudden we had to work our way back up the pecking order while being careful you didn't get run off. A lot of awfully good players who were players under Bass's regime left the team by choice or were run off. A good forty percent of the scholarship players left between the spring of 1966 to the spring of 1967. The new staff did things differently than the previous staff. This new staff felt we were not playing to our ability. Initially they made things extremely tough. Rules, rules and more rules. They were definitely trying to get rid of players they felt weren't playing up to their abilities on and off the practice field. Coach Dietzel's coaching style was a lot different than Coach Bass's. I guess the biggest difference was Coach Bass treated us like men with simple rules. Coach Dietzel had a rule for everything from getting up for breakfast to making your bed and keeping your room clean. He was a lot more structured about the small things. It was hard for some of the players to grasp this off-field discipline. On the field practices were much more physical. At first you truly felt that he was weeding out and wanted to cut down on numbers, then build the team back up with his new recruits.

Coach Dietzel was also named Athletic Director and he discovered that we supposedly had an ineligible player on the roster and we forfeited our share of the ACC Championship even though this ineligible player never played a down.

Our record was 5-5 and they never officially changed that. I rebelled. I never turned my gold football back that read 1965 ACC Co-champions. I felt we won it fair and square on the field and I was honored to play on that team as a sophomore with a lot of great teammates. It was a wild finish to an already long winter and spring practice and a lot of things changed.

Well, like Coach Moss said, "Stay eligible, work hard and things will always work out." I don't know if it at first was a form of motivation, but initially the new staff made a lot of guys feel unwanted. With some, this form of motivation didn't work and we lost a lot of good players. With me, it made me want to prove him and my position coach wrong. I remember my defensive line coach the first day of practice saying, "Half of you won't be here for our first game." And he was right.

We went from sixteen defensive linemen to seven before the start of the '66 season. We went from a very promising season to a disappointing one. We left a lot on the preseason practice field. Initially a lot of players transferred, got run off, or just quit college football. At first this new staff wasn't much fun to be around and they chased off a lot of very promising players. Why? Who knows?

The 1966 season was a difficult year. We won one game and lost nine. The reasons for such a bad year were placed mostly on the players. We were told we were lazy, poor students, and just overall not any good and in order to turn the program around we needed a complete makeover and once our attitude changed things would improve.

Remember, during the first half of spring practice in 1966 we felt we were going to be the team to beat in the ACC with all that we had returning. But due to injuries, players either leaving on their own or being run off by the new staff, we were a shell of the team that if the Bass staff stayed in place would have contended for the Championship.

At the end of the '66 season with a loss to Clemson at Clemson, everyone in the locker room was committed to the hard work ahead of us to get back on a winning track.

Prior to the 1967 season, after a grueling five-day-a-week offseason program and a real tough spring practice, we finally started to become a team, both players and coaches.

The players finally wanted to be there again and the staff liked coaching the ones who had stuck it out. The initial shock of the new staff's coaching style of pushing us to the limit and seeing who survived was over.

I had a great training partner, Joe Komoroski, who was a real beast on the field and in the weight room. We were good for each other because if either one of us didn't go full speed, the other one would definitely push the one who wasn't.

By the time we lined up for our first game versus Iowa State in 1967, we were in great shape and probably as strong, or stronger, than our opponents. Coach Jones, our defensive line coach, sure used our intensity against each other to set the tone for our defensive practice.

In the season of 1967, we got off to a 3-0 start. Our offense was banged up a little, especially at the running back position. We lost two very good backs prior to the start of the season, a big fullback named Jimmy Killen and one of the best I ever saw, Benny Galloway. With those two in the backfield along with Ben Garnto, we would have had a backfield as good as any of our opponents especially with a young sophomore named Warren Muir. It was sure difficult playing Florida State, Georgia, and Alabama with a banged up offensive backfield.

During the l967 season there was a lot going on in the world, but playing major college football and going to class took the majority of my time and focus. Two things that still stand out in my mind, and really depict the atmosphere of the mid-sixties, were the racial tension and the Vietnam War.

The racial tension came to a head in Winston-Salem and throughout the country the weekend we played Wake Forest. We were supposed to play them Saturday afternoon, but wound up playing them Sunday night under guarded conditions while the riots were going on and many cities were having major problems among the black and white communities. We lost a tough game plus we lost our opportunity to play in the Sun Bowl following our final game defeat to Clemson at home.

It was a little depressing not to go to a bowl game. But, I felt extremely lucky to be in college playing football and getting a good education while a lot of young men who were my age were fighting in Vietnam so guys like me could be home enjoying the freedoms that they were fighting for. I was extremely thankful for what they were doing.

I received some post season honors, but would have traded them all for another shot at Wake. But life went on. I was honored to be named to the All-Atlantic Coast Conference defensive team along with an honorable mention to the Associated Press All-American Team.

But the biggest thrill and honor was to be named co-captain along with Joe Komoroski of 1967 Gamecock football. This position was voted on by our teammates and to this day was one of my greatest athletic achievements.

FOUR

After my senior season of college football, I thought about playing professionally and was offered a few opportunities. But, because I played as a true sophomore, I needed another year to obtain my diploma along with asking my "sweetheart," Susan Dillon, to marry me.

We were making plans to get married in the summer of 1968. Financially, between my stipend for coaching, and doing weight training seminars for Universal Gym part time, plus my summer work up north, I would make considerably more money than I would have made attempting to play football on the next level. The decision was an easy one. I decided not to accept the opportunity to continue my playing career but to go back to college, get my diploma and accept the opportunity to be a graduate assistant and start my coaching career, something I knew I would always wind up doing.

My coaching career started during the long offseason conditioning program of 1968 and continued through spring practice. I realized that spring that this was the profession I wanted to be associated with, especially when a young defensive tackle I was working with called me "Coach." I so wanted to deserve that title. I wanted to pass things on to my players that I had learned.

The number one way that I improved as a player was to use every method possible to learn. I let them know you learn first from listening and being told how to do what is needed from you, then develop your skills. Secondly you learn from watching, may it be films or the man in front of you in line getting his turn to do a drill, observe the technique and mentally critique it, and finally you learn by doing—practice and perfect the techniques needed.

It was so rewarding to use my work ethic as a player to help direct the energy of these peers, now players, as a new coach. They remembered that I was an over-achiever as a player and played far above my potential. I helped them realize early on that it was about performance not potential. I worked very hard to get the young players to realize what I learned from my position coaches, to work at improving their abilities to play every rep. I got them to want to improve every practice. I wanted them to enjoy the competition, understand the importance of always giving it your maximum effort, doing everything with a purpose from the beginning of practice to hanging up your equipment in your locker when it was over.

An important coaching philosophy was being developed. It was a coach's responsibility to help the person you're working with to get better each rep—each day in everything they are involved with. It was important to me that I was creating an environment that they wanted to be part of. This environment was similar to the environment that the masons I used to work with created on the jobsite. Everything had a purpose. Everyone was important. We all were taught to enjoy the environment and do a good job. The harder you worked the easier the task at hand became for everyone.

During that spring I was starting to develop my own coaching concepts. Like a good mason building a foundation, I was building a solid coaching philosophy. My coaching foundation was built on these three simple concepts. First, I wanted them to <u>want</u> to be at practice. Second, I wanted them to <u>enjoy</u> everything about it, and finally I wanted them to learn to <u>compete</u> against their own abilities and work to <u>improve</u> on these abilities every minute they were on the practice field.

As a coach, I wanted to be a leader, not a manager. In sign language the sign for manager looks like one is pulling the reins of a horse. For a leader the sign is cuddling a baby in your arms. This is the perfect definition of a leader.

After the summer break, I returned to USC a married man, and my wife, Susan, was expecting our first child. My priorities changed. I didn't have much free time. Between working with Universal Gym, going to class and coaching, the semester flew by. Coaching was my escape time. I really loved it. I enjoyed everything about it.

The fall of 1968 found me coaching the USC defensive line at the freshman level. The Head Coach of the freshman team was a veteran coach named "Pride" Ratterree. He was a great man to be around. His nickname "Pride" really depicted his personality. He was a wonderful person to learn from. He helped me to understand the total game. The little free time I had I was spending watching film and stealing time from the varsity position coaches. The game as far as X's and O's really intrigued me. I was adding to my coaching foundation.

Football is a game that really isn't as complex as some people make it. On defense I learned "shame on you" if you're out-flanked and you'd better "play defense on the other side of the ball," "attack—attack." On offense, "block the right guy and maintain contact," and "give the running back lanes."

The 1968 football season flew by and we went undefeated. We dominated our opponents especially on defense. The one thing I enjoyed most was the positive relationship I developed with those players who were only four or five years younger than I.

Initially I enjoyed coaching almost as much as playing. I began to realize football is a game where everyone has individual responsibilities and collectively the team works for victory. The more I coached the more I felt involved in this effort. It didn't take long to feel that "yes" I was still playing but just a different position. Now I was playing the position called coach.

One of the reasons why I enjoy going back to games at Carolina some forty years later is how those players introduce me to their friends and family. They introduce me as "their coach" especially the defensive line guys and collectively we remember how hard we worked each rep in order to compete with the toughest competition—"Self."

After the season was over and I finally graduated in January, 1969, I decided to move back to New Jersey; first to help my in-laws run a family restaurant and tavern business, and more importantly I wanted our child to be around our extended family.

The next year went by fast. During that year I started up my own property maintenance company, bought a house and started looking for a teaching and coaching job.

My high school baseball and business mentor, Frank Vicendese, was now the Vice Principal of Dunellen High School and was about to leave education to run his family business full time. Coincidentally, Dunellen was my wife, Susan's, hometown and one of my high school's big rivals.

Dunellen was having a very difficult time fielding a football team and wrestling team. A lot of discussion was going on to drop both programs. At the end of the 1969-70 school year there were approximately fourteen players on the football team with a third of them being seniors. The wrestling team finished their season with only six student athletes and neither team won a game or match that season, and had not done so for quite some time.

It was late June, 1970, when Frank called me about the potential position at Dunellen. I told him I had already accepted an assistant coaching position in three sports along with a teaching job at a big Group IV school, but I would come in and talk about the Dunellen situation. The superintendent, Dr. Goldstein, was in favor of doing away with both programs. Because of some pressure by a few parents, Frank convinced him to talk with me before he made such an important decision about altering the school's athletic programs.

FIVE

After three very long meetings with the Dunellen High School superintendent, principal and board president, they decided to create a new teaching position for me along with naming me both head football and wrestling coach. It was a one-year opportunity. There was no promise of keeping either or both programs after this one-year commitment.

After talking with the athletic director and a few parents, I decided to accept this challenging opportunity. I felt very good about administrative and family support. I realized very early on in my coaching career that the more people you have on the same page regarding how you are going to achieve a goal, the less difficult this achievement becomes. Collectively, we decided that our goal would be to field a competitive team, improve upon the players' academic and social behavior, along with helping these students continue their education and athletic participation by obtaining scholarships. The decision was an easy one. I accepted it and had six weeks to get ready for our first practice.

The league was extremely difficult and very competitive playing local powers, Roselle Park, Middlesex and Kenilworth, along with Immaculata, the largest parochial school in our area. Dunellen had one of the smallest school enrollments in New Jersey that had a football team, which added to the tough task of developing a competitive and disciplined team, but the decision was made and there was no turning back.

I remember distinctly my first experience talking to the press as a head football coach when the reporter asked me what I was going to do first, now that I accepted the job. I blurted out this long run-on sentence. "I have to put a staff together, recruit players, improve the facilities and equipment, meet the faculty, meet the parents, develop an offensive, defensive and kicking game playbook, work on getting a weight room, and set up a pre-school study hall."

I was getting both tired and excited just thinking about all the things we had to do. You had to see the look on the sportswriter's face. This was all coming from a twenty-three year old who had never been a head coach—working to develop a program that hadn't won a game in a couple of years, plus at the time there weren't too many if any local high schools that had a weight room or used weights as a method to improve strength and speed, so why should we?

Along with all of this, my first daughter, Gretchen, was going to have a sister who was going to be born right in the middle of the football season. Yes, my second daughter, Heidi, was born three hours after the sixth game that first season. I moved into a new house and was running my own construction business. I had to run my life like a practice schedule. Every hour, every minute, every second had to be accounted for. I knew time was a gift from our Lord and what I did with it in His name was my gift back but, boy, was I busy.

I was officially appointed to the position of driver education instructor and coach at the July school board meeting and it was now official and I could begin work. Mike Shello, the athletic director, said there would be three paid positions available for assistant coaches if we could field a varsity team. If we couldn't field a varsity team and chose to play a junior varsity team schedule only, I would be allowed to have two paid assistants.

Along with this, as the head coach in wrestling I would have no assistants initially, but if the program grew I may have one down the line. Well, along with putting a staff together my next priority was to meet with every male in the high school. With only approximately a hundred boys, this took me just a week to talk with all of them.

I had three open meetings initially with maybe fifteen students showing up in total. But the word was getting around. My next method of getting to them was the phone, followed by home visits and going to the local hangouts. I compiled a list of potential players and while I was compiling this list I was also taking notes on why they didn't want to be involved with the football program and what they felt was wrong with it.

By listening to all of the negatives, I was developing a positive game plan and the interest in being involved was growing by both students and parents. I became a good listener and the students' reasons for not being involved or what had to be fixed were all things that were not insurmountable.

The number one reason for not playing was no one wanted to be involved with a program that had a losing stigma attached to it. The second reason was the poor equipment and outdated facilities. I promised this all would change starting with new equipment and uniforms. I told them individually, with their support, the "wins" would come and respect would be earned. They saw my commitment and felt my energy and knew I would take care of my end of the bargain. But, I needed players. Slowly, but surely, I knew I would find players who would help me improve the image of the football program.

Dunellen had a great basketball tradition, so the athletes were there. What I had to do was get those athletes to play football. The recruiting process was in full swing and within a few weeks sixteen upperclassmen and five freshmen said they would definitely play and another three upperclassmen and four freshmen were maybes. I showed this list to the Athletic Director and he said go ahead and find three assistants. It looked like we had a good shot at fielding a varsity team, so we kept our two-tier varsity-junior varsity schedule in place.

I sent out a questionnaire to the existing faculty and no one had any interest in coaching football. There still were half a dozen teaching openings and the administration promised they would do their best to give priority to those who had coaching backgrounds when hiring new teachers. These three positions were filled by teachers who said they would coach football. Out of the three, only one had coaching experience. His experience was one year coaching on the freshman level.

Now we had staff and players. The next three items that we had to do were improve the facilities, put our playbooks together and quickly try to upgrade the equipment.

We met as a staff three nights a week preparing for the season. I met with as many players as possible, working out with them to improve their strength and speed. It was fun working out with them. There was no better way than teaching them by example. A lot of my friends, from the Plainfield Gym where I worked out as a player, enjoyed coming over and working out with our players.

Our equipment was mostly donated by these hard core lifters who loved seeing these young kids getting hooked on this "new" concept of weight training. After the workouts, we would spend a couple hours cleaning up, repairing the showers and painting the field house.

Each morning I would set up a creeper watering system that I borrowed from a farmer who I knew, to try to get some grass to grow on our field that looked more like a dirt car track than a football field. Progress was being made, and over a five-week stretch, improvements on the negatives were visible.

Organized practice in New Jersey in the early seventies started after Labor Day. At our first practice we had twenty-four players in uniform. The attitude was super. They were proud of themselves because we had won our first big challenge.

We were going to field a varsity team. We had increased our participation by sixty percent over last year's first day turnout.

We also had a student manager who I had attend a student training camp in August as both equipment manager and my assistant trainer. I was not only head football coach, but trainer and head groundskeeper. If everything wasn't in order, my student manager/trainer would remind me what things had to be done. Over my tenure at Dunellen, Joe Brennan was my right hand man. He helped me with all aspects. His commitment was limitless.

Joe was a great human being who really loved Dunellen football. After high school, Joe volunteered his services to the next four football coaches and did a great job for them also. Joe died at a young age but will always be remembered by those players and coaches that he helped, doing something that he truly loved, helping the Dunellen football program.

By the fourth Saturday of September, the night of our first game, we finally had some semblance of a football team especially wearing our new game jerseys that our parents' club purchased for us. We looked pretty good the day before our first game when we took the 1970 team picture. All twenty-four candidates from our first practice were now proud members of our varsity team.

On the bus ride to our first game, you could hear a pin drop. We were playing Immaculata High School, a big Catholic school who beat up on Dunellen years prior.

After playing way above our heads for the first three and a half quarters, the score was 0-0. Needless to say, everyone was in shock that we were playing so well including our opponent. Our last drive stalled and we turned the ball over on downs to Immaculata on their own fifteen yard line with less than two minutes remaining in the game.

We held them for three downs and it was now fourth down and three. The clock was stopped because on the previous play the runner ran out of bounds. When Immaculata came out and lined up in a three wide set for their final play, we called time out. This was their favorite passing formation and I was betting that they were going to go deep. If they were going to gamble, so would we.

39

I went into the defensive huddle and I told the kids we were going to get into our ten man punt block formation. Immaculata had no timeouts left and just twenty ticks left on the clock. You should have seen the looks on our kids' faces. Some were looks of disbelief and some were biting their lips so they wouldn't burst out laughing because they really believed it would work and were truly buying in. Rushing ten men we would definitely have them outnumbered. Our guys really got excited and felt that they could get to the quarterback for sure before he threw it deep. They knew this wasn't a normal thing to do, but football is a game of surprises.

When Immaculata came to the line of scrimmage, we shifted into our ten man punt block at the snap. As the quarterback got the ball and dropped back to throw, our kids broke through the line. Immaculata didn't have enough men to block us. As our players came through clean they were coached to scream and yell. If we didn't get to the quarterback we hoped we would at least scare him.

As he dropped back, he was outnumbered. Four players broke clean. He started running backward to avoid the rush and before he was about to be tackled in the end zone, he threw the ball away avoiding the sack. He didn't realize that throwing the ball away in the end zone was a penalty with the result being a safety.

Truthfully, when I first saw the flag, I wasn't sure what was happening. There definitely was a hush in the stadium. After a brief meeting and no time left on the clock, the head official signaled a safety. We were awarded two points and the victory. The streak was over. Dunellen won.

To this day I don't know how many people, other than our football family, realized how important that victory was. I really believe that safety saved the Dunellen football program and gave a lot of great kids the chance to be a Destroyer and wear their letterman jackets with pride. All season long we played way above our heads and all of our seniors who wanted to continue their football careers did so. Our record was 2-6-1, but the W's and L's were no measuring stick for how successful that season was. Not only did all our kids finish the season, but three seniors were awarded full football scholarships with one of them being named to the Group I All-State Team. Pride in the football program had finally returned, returned to a program that sportswriters used to write jokes about.

After a decent winter program in which all of our returning players either played basketball or wrestling, it was time to really improve on our facilities.

Going back to when Dr. Goldstein, the Superintendent of Schools, offered me the coaching job, he said he would create a teaching position in Driver Education, knowing we didn't have a car yet. Because of this I had time to do what I thought was important. I told him I would have a new 1971 Toyota donated by April and an idea how we could renovate the field house and add on an exercise/team room at no cost to the town or school district. After a meeting with the mayor, principal, superintendent and athletic director, we all felt it was a great idea—an offer "we" couldn't refuse. So, collectively we decided to go for it.

The first thing we had to do was to get some plans and get them okayed by the building code offices. With everyone working together we pulled out some old favors and got this done in a week.

While that was going on, I got commitments for all the material needed. Now we started working the press and got publicity on what was going on because it was a positive. Thank God for some good friends who were in the building supply business who donated the material and found me some masons to do the block work for free. We knew enough about construction to complete an addition to this antiquated building and turn it into a very useful facility.

Along with the skilled labor who was donating time I needed a labor force. The principal allowed me to use student/athletes during their study hall and physical education classes during the week. On weekends between friends, family, fans, and players, we really had too many, but who cared. It was a party and we were getting it done.

41

We completed the job before graduation. During the period of April to June, our booster club ran fundraisers and made enough money to outfit this area with exercise equipment. Finally the showers and toilets worked. That summer we had one of the first exclusive high school weight rooms—members only—and the athletes had keys to prove it. Supervision was bountiful and the parents helped enforce the luxury. That room was used as a weight room, wrestling practice area/ team room. But it was a special place "game day" at Dunellen for thirty plus years until finally a player who I had the privilege to coach became teacher, coach and finally administrator and just recently good old Columbia Park got a "major" makeover. Good job, David DeNapoli.

While all this was going on, we put our academic and social improvement program in place. The faculty was great. We were all friends wanting to make things better and help the students learn. We built a triangle with the student/athlete in the middle. Of course the parents were the major driving force. What a wonderful group of people they were. Everyone bought in and our line of communication was almost flawless.

A great story comes to mind when I think of this. One of our players wasn't doing his job in the classroom preparing for a final exam his junior year. After the math teacher notified me, I knew the student had early dismissal to give him time to go home and study. I decided to keep this student with me. My office was a six by ten renovated closet with a window that was two stories up. It was located in the gym, extremely out of the way.

I put him in there after lunch and told him I'd be back in a few hours, "So, study." I came back in about thirty minutes later to check on him and he was in the gym shooting hoops. That was it! My veins swelled up and I went to the moon.

This time I put him in there, closed and locked the door from the outside, forgetting to flip the fan switch from the outside. There was no fan switch inside the study area/office/storage closet.

We had a faculty meeting which lasted almost two hours on the topic of the end of the school year procedure. After the meeting, some teachers stopped at the Dunellen Hotel, the local hangout where you could get a good lunch. About two hours later, I realized I had forgotten about him.

I took care of my bill and immediately left. While driving back to school I was having nightmares. I rushed into the building and unlocked the door. As I opened it, he ran out like a poor dog that was penned up on a hot summer day with no water yelling, "I promise I'll study and make good grades." It was hard for me to keep a straight face and show no emotion, especially laughter. I bit my lip and said, "I hope you learned your lesson." Down deep inside I was thanking God he hadn't fainted from heat stroke.

The next three school years went fast and every student who wanted to go to college got the opportunity to do so. We had three Division I scholarships and a couple IAA scholarships along with a handful of NAIA and Division III football grant and needs scholarships.

In the winter of 1973 we built a new wrestling room because now we had a three tier program and we were winning a heck of a lot more than we were losing. And given that we now had two driver education cars, one for the new superintendent to drive home and the other for me to drive home, it was pretty cool having a company car. Things were definitely on pace.

We now had a three-tier program in football—freshmen, junior varsity and varsity—along with a nice feeding Pop Warner program and we were competitive on all levels in both football and wrestling. People finally had to take Dunellen seriously and our kids always felt they could win every time we lined up or had a wrestling match.

I believe our eleven wins in wrestling in 1973 still is the most dual meet wins in Dunellen's school history. That wrestling season was extremely rewarding because in a short time we went from one of the worst programs in central New Jersey to a team that had to be respected and sometimes feared.

In the spring of 1974, I started to look in the state paper at potential coaching jobs. I checked out things and thought about maybe moving on to a larger district. Also I wanted to at least start to get some experience with the total interviewing process and learn from it.

Well, that beautiful saying, "Seek and ye shall find." As I looked I found a new opportunity and saying goodbye to the Dunellen community and student body was an extremely positive experience, even though initially a few of the young guys were mad at me. Thank God that didn't last long. Everyone realized I was making a very good career move.

After it was official that I was leaving following the third marking period, which was only a few weeks away, they surprised me with a party. This wonderful booster club also used this farewell party as a fundraiser. The money raised that night bought football sweat outfits for the returning players, which was now close to thirty.

I was humbled because the parents were thanking me. I told them it should be reversed. I should be the one thanking them for teaching me how important it was for everyone to communicate collectively so we could reach a common goal.

I should be thanking the faculty for allowing me to learn that if we all worked together, teacher-coach-parent, improvements would be made.

The lesson of 'do your best all the time' was so important. I really believe from my experiences you must win in the classroom because this success affects why a team wins more than any other possible reason.

The administration at Dunellen was special. At the time we didn't realize that we were probably one of the first schools in the state to have an on-the-job training program. Teaching our student athletes how to paint, do masonry work, carpentry work and anything else necessary to build and maintain a weight room and wrestling area was unique, but so was almost everything we did.

I followed the careers and lives of most all the students I had the opportunity to work with at Dunellen. These skills we learned off the field helped a lot of them in their career paths after high school.

It was also a training program for my construction company. At least a half dozen kids who were involved with me improving the facilities at Dunellen worked for me for years and later had their own businesses using the skills that we learned working together those years.

You learn from doing. I was allowed to do a lot of different things during my tenure there. These lessons learned were definitely going to be used in a new and exciting opportunity.

SIX

The opportunity to teach in a school system such as North Hunterdon Regional, at the time the largest sending district in the state with a five star educational reputation, was too much to turn down. I could not have done anything except accept the job. Being an assistant in both football and wrestling for one year, then the second year, be a head in one and an assistant in the other, or if need be the head of both was just too much to turn down along with a nice pay increase.

I began my tenure there just as the fourth marking period was starting in the spring of 1974. Teaching physical education was really a great profession. During a nine period day, I was assigned five teaching classes, two duties, and prep time. If you were a head coach, they assigned you prep time at the end of the day. They gave me that courtesy which allowed sufficient time to prepare for practice.

My teaching schedule could not have been better. Every class was different. My responsibilities were three physical education classes all being different grade levels, one special needs class, and one weight room. North Hunterdon Regional had a beautifully and intelligently designed fitness area. The room was paid for by a state-funded program. We definitely took advantage of this pilot program. It was a luxury to have such a classroom.

My responsibility in football was defensive coordinator and I also was responsible for setting up a strength and speed program. Fritz Halfacre, a legend in eastern Pennsylvania and Western Jersey because of his reputation for quickly resurrecting programs, was named the head coach and what a "boss" he was. He was a true "professor" of the game of football with a strong and unique grasp of all aspects of the high school game. Along with this opportunity to work with Fritz, my wrestling assignment was to work with the upper weight classes and introduce new strength and conditioning concepts for a Hall of Fame coach named Harry Vandermark. The new district high school construction had already started and would open the following school year and one or maybe both programs' head coaching positions would be assigned to me.

It was a long time since North had more wins than losses in football. Baseball and track were good programs but wrestling was definitely number one. Wrestling had so much power that the school's varsity football schedule was only eight weeks long compared to nine or ten weeks long at other schools prior to playoffs. They did this so the wrestlers would have a two and a half week jump on their opponents. Wrestling was definitely number one.

All the coaches bought into a new philosophy that the best out-of-season program was to play another sport. Finally we got the basketball coach to buy in and the basketball players were now also playing football. We really liked the athletes to play at least two sports. If they didn't, we had an intramural program year round which included speed and strength along with competitive games. Our intramural floor hockey league became very popular among the students and it was attracting fans. Convincing the athletes to participate in more than one sport or specializing in one sport was similar in all the schools I coached in. You had to get the athletes to believe that the best out-of-season program was to play another sport. By doing this all sports improved instead of one improving at another's expense.

It was like gaining a Master's degree in coaching being a part of turning North Hunterdon from a cellar dweller into a championship football program. The first thing that was instilled was all things needed to be done in a very organized manner, from recognizing problems to coming up with a game plan or solution, and then following through on this decision. It was full speed ahead with all involved contributing their best effort.

A very strong football frame of mind was developing among the athletes because they were surrounded with a feeling of strong commitment from the coaching staff and support groups. We coached whomever and wherever we could.

The physical education department head and faculty helped by just being great teachers—we had a strong commitment in our teaching philosophy which was to improve athletic skills and competitive spirit in our four-day a week physical education curriculum based on each student's needs. This wasn't a roll the ball out mentality. Everything had a purpose. Students loved physical education. For most, it was a high point of the day. Competition was preached and talents and skills were learned and developed. Also on the fifth day of rotation we had a study hall program in which we initiated our once a week academic progress report system, so we were constantly monitoring both academic and athletic improvement.

Without this communication and ability to work together as a faculty, we never would have achieved success so quickly. North's Athletic Director was a very strong leader and always said in order to be a good coach you had to be a good teacher. There was an awful lot of pride at North to do a good job in the classroom and in any extracurricular activity that you chose to be involved in. The physical education teacher at North was accepted by the rest of the faculty as a professional.

Our first summer, we had an open gym concept which was strictly volunteer. Both the coaches and athletes volunteered their time. We had a wrestling clinic going on simultaneously with a basketball clinic. We integrated speed and strength improvement into both clinics. At the end of these two clinics, that lasted an hour or so, we had a forty-five minute football clinic. By doing it this way we had access to all of the athletes. There is always a reason behind the method.

People were noticing how hard we were working to make our athletes better. Some of the support groups around the building started to catch on to the improved and more competitive attitude. Competition, competition in everything we did. This mindset was starting to pay off. We were having fun making a game out of everything from grades to playing chess to a volleyball game. Always compete. Someone must win. Someone must not. It sure was more fun winning.

The groundskeepers and custodians were major contributors to the fast turn-around and became important members of our football family. These men and women would do anything that we asked of them. Boy, what a luxury. After a long day at school during football season that would start at six a.m. and end at seven or eight p. m., the groundscrew would have a cold beer ready along with something good to eat to hold you over until you got home for a late night supper.

1974 really was a magical year and we had a 7-1 season in football. Fritz did a masterful job convincing everyone that the will to compete—to compete to win—was so very important. His goal was to have our seniors enjoy a successful final year. He really made sure no one became complacent about playing to win. I realized a good lesson.

By the end of the first season our play was slipping. The wrestlers on the team lost concentration. This lack of concentration or switch of concentration came to a head the beginning of November when some of the wrestlers were wearing sweat gear, those rubberized tops and bottoms which kids used to drop weight. We were having a conflict with a few players about this issue and finally the staff came to an agreement. No sweat gear at practice. We did our best to keep their focus, but this was wrestling country.

This situation of lack of concentration almost caused us to lose an important game two years later when I was the head football coach. After starting out great we were playing our seventh game of the season. The new wrestling coach decided to have a pre-season wrestling tournament for non-football participants and use our football players as scorekeepers the night before our game. The following day we were getting beat halftime by a team who we should have been handling. As we were leaving the field, my special ed students were cheering as though we were winning.

Walking into the locker room, I told my assistants what I was going to do. I was going to leave and sit with my special ed students because they believed we could win and their mind was on the game. The players were shocked because half time was a time I would go over how we were playing and make adjustments accordingly. Fifteen minutes later, they came out of the locker room a much better focused team and we won the game going away. Point made—you must stay focused on the task at hand.

As I stated earlier, teaching and coaching at North was a learning situation. As a young coach, I was always seeking information. It's tough to be "original" but as a coach you must use everything available to pull off a decision. One of the things that was a major improvement in my coaching philosophy was to act, instead of react. I learned when you act you think about your decision of what to do and when you react you do exactly that—just react, you don't think first.

A funny example of acting was in 1979 when we returned to the State Championship Playoffs. Our first game was against the number one ranked team in our bracket. No one gave us a chance to win. Some papers had us as a four touchdown underdog. Plus, the bus ride was two hours away. I asked Bob to come to practice that Monday with the travel plans. We decided he was going to send us on the school buses with bag lunches. I told Bob I would rally the kids and boycott such arrangements and demand better. It was a sight to watch Bob Hopek, our Athletic Director, the players and me negotiating two nice cruiser buses, a breakfast at the local diner before leaving, and a real post game meal at a restaurant after the game before heading home. We used this as a starting point for a great week of practice. We played a beautiful game and out-toughed our opponents to reach the state finals. It's great to act.

The administration, faculty and parental support was extraordinary. They saw the fruits of our labor so quickly. It really was amazing when everybody was on the same page to make a goal become a reality. Wow, it was a party after every athletic event at "Smigelsky's," a great bar and eatery with a world class jukebox. Coaches, faculty, family members and locals loved the winning atmosphere and good food and drink. A lot of good ideas got their start on a Smigelsky's Bar napkin.

Once the football season was over, it was wrestling season. About fifty percent of our wrestlers were football participants our first year. Now I saw them in a new surrounding. "The Wrestling Room" was a different environment.

Head Coach Harry Vandermark definitely knew his kids' limitations. He knew just how hard he could push each wrestler. More than in any sport I've ever been around, no one had to make a commitment like a wrestler did back in the sixties and seventies. Wrestling was unique. Not only did you have the physical demands of the sport, but you also had to maintain a certain weight. Personal grooming was also governed. The wrestlers' hair had to be kept neat and above the ears. No facial hair was allowed.

Wrestling season was almost as long and hard as Harry's practices. We started the second week of November and our last day of practice was the beginning of March. You had practices through two vacation weeks. Boy, it was tough on everybody. But on the bright side, my two girls and wife loved it. They loved the excitement of the home meets and coming to practice and helping out. Most of all I think they really enjoyed the fun at Smigelsky's after many big wins.

Spring finally came and Hunterdon County was a good place to be. You were surrounded with great trout fishing, from creeks, to streams and rivers and finally lake or reservoir fishing and my students and players were showing "Coach" all the best spots.

That spring we documented who was playing spring sports and who wasn't. We, with the help of a great physical education department, made sure all our football athletes were constantly improving strength and speed. For those who wanted to, we had a great competitive three-day a week intramural program. We did something different every time.

An example of the three-day schedule would be hockey (no skates), lacrosse and kickball-dodge ball. We did this in our padded auxiliary gym. It was nuts. We were definitely building a lot of positives, especially toughness.

Hunterdon County is a beautiful place and we did a lot of fun things together from jumping off bridges into the river to following the trout stocking truck to some secret fishing spots. Summer went fast and I was ready for our second year, together with my new titles.

SEVEN

Wow, titles. Along with titles came responsibility and accountability at North Hunterdon Regional. During the school day, Fritz was at our new sister school, Voorhees High School. He was promoted to Head of the Guidance Department. Voorhees was only going to have a junior varsity football program. So for a lot of reasons my new title was co-head coach and defensive coordinator. After this season, I would be named head football coach.

Along with my new football title, I was also named the head wrestling coach. I was very excited about my two new positions including the responsibilities. It was great as long as you won. If you didn't, you figured out what was broken and fixed it real quick. If you didn't, Mr. Hopek wanted to know why.

Our Athletic Director, Bob Hopek, was a wonderful athletic director to work for. We didn't always agree on every issue but one way or another, the problem would be solved and a decision would be made. Usually these decisions were made after a good discussion. Sometimes they were made on the wrestling mat. Yes, we would shoot takedowns against each other with the winner getting his way. But in the end, Bob was the "Boss" and a better one would be hard to find.

The 1975 season got off to a great start. We were 5-0 and we weren't challenged yet. We were constantly scrutinizing our performance always finding ways to do it better on and off the field.

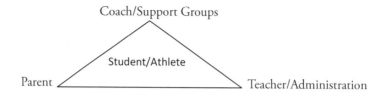

Coach/Support Groups

Student/Athlete

Parent   Teacher/Administration

Our support triangle, that we liked keeping our athletes in, was in place and working well. All we had to do was make sure all three corners communicated and this concept worked. The problems were the same, but the reasons for those problems changed from school district to school district.

Our sixth game was against Hackettstown High School, a rural school like ours, but with a little street attitude. They had a reputation of being a very tough physical group year after year. We were getting good state press and were a couple of touchdown favorites. During the first quarter and halfway through the second quarter we had some key turnovers inside our own twenty yard line leading to scores by Hackettstown. After the third score, Fritz ran over to me and asked me what was wrong with the defense. I started stating that the defense wasn't even on the field for two of the scores. Before I knew it he smacked me in the back of the head with "love" and said, "I wasn't looking for excuses. I am looking for solutions."

What I did next became a classic in North Hunterdon folklore.

I put a team bench on the fifty yard line perpendicular to the sidelines and told him you stay on your side and take care of the offense, and I'll stay on my side and I'll make sure they don't score another point. Well, it worked on defense. We stopped them cold. And our offense did great. We won the game four scores to three.

Our kids rallied around both of us after they witnessed firsthand the "Fritz and Don Show." Thank God for the thought process of think first then act instead of "reacting" without thinking. In my life there were times I reacted and the majority of those actions were costly and were often wrong.

Next game up was Hunterdon Central who was also undefeated at the time. The Devils for the last five meetings really gave us a whipping especially in 1974 when they rubbed it in a little.

We had to find a way to give our kids a war cry—a theme—a torch to carry, anything to give us an edge. After a great coaches' meeting at Smig's after our Sunday film breakdown, we had a few ideas. Fritz, Bob Hopek and Bud Vanetta, our superintendent in charge of buildings and grounds, came up with a winner. We loved his suggestion.

We decided to send our own team flowers. We also painted the front entrance way to our field house with a washable paint, stating how sorry they (Hunterdon Central) were going to be for ruining our homecoming dance.

The theme of proving ourselves the better team was carried out in front of the biggest crowd ever to watch a high school football game in Hunterdon County. We beat a very good football team to go 7-0 and won our last game to finish our year 8-0. Now we had two weeks to prepare for our first state playoff game.

The on-the-field playoff system in New Jersey was just beginning and still in its infant stages. All of the guidelines weren't completely spelled out. How true an old saying—"Where there is confusion, there is gain"—played out. As a coach I always knew breaking down film, I mean really dissecting them, was so valuable. Now the ability to obtain films became a trump card. The sectional seating would come out on Monday. That gave us two days to get a jump on our opponent. So through the process of elimination we narrowed down our opponent to three potential teams. Coaches are a very tight fraternity. So by ten p.m. Saturday night, I had two films on each opponent from opposing coaches of those teams. By Sunday night, I had all films broken down and ready for our six p.m. coaching meeting.

I really loved those coaching staff meetings at North. We used to debate and at times have a good honest to God argument trying to put game plans together that would give us an edge. Our goal was to win the State Championship one game at a time. We were seeded third and our opponent, the second-seeded team, was also undefeated. They were definitely the favorite according to the state paper—a three or four touchdown favorite. They outweighed our line by about fifty pounds minimum per man and had great team speed. Facts were facts. We could not change those facts, but we built our game plan with the concept of taking advantage of our opponent's strengths and weaknesses.

We devised our game plan using blocking angles, trapping and play action passes. Our defensive concept was to be very offensive. We worked hard on gap control and beating our much larger opponents off the line of scrimmage. Our goal was to play defense on their side of the line of scrimmage. So after some very positive debate, which was the only way to utilize everyone's opinion, we all felt very positive about our concept. Now it was time to convince everyone involved to buy in.

Coaching is like selling. You definitely have to communicate and be humble in your delivery getting the message across. Once we had everyone on the same page, the next step was pulling it off. With the help of administration, faculty, support staffs, coaches, managers, players, band director, cheerleaders, student body, parents and community, we beat the number two seed and the number one seed and fulfilled our dream to become state champs and to be ranked among the state's top teams. It was both a happy time and a sad time. It took us only two years to bring a school and community together to build a state caliber program. At the end of the 1976 school year, our second year, the school would be officially divided with half staying at North and the other half attending the new school. The deciding factor would be what area of the county the student lived in.

Over the following three years, I was both a head coach in football and wrestling. We won seventy percent of our games and again played for the state championship in football in 1978, losing in the finals.

One of the many things we accomplished at North during my tenure there was the amount of young men who went on and played college football. Approximately twenty-five continued their careers and received college diplomas with a third of them playing Division I or IAA football, and one of them, Dave Smigelsky, played professionally with the Seattle Seahawks. The era between 1974 and 1979 was North's glory days in football, making it to the playoffs three times. When I think why, I come up with many reasons.

- A great staff who had the ability to argue and debate in a very positive way and, once a decision was made, we all bought in and carried out this decision.
- Strong support from faculty and board employees including maintenance and cafeteria staff. Along with this wonderful group, the community was 100 percent behind us, especially our booster members.
- Bonding off-field relationships between coaches and players.
- No jealousy between coaches—a definite one for all and all for one attitude.

Why would anyone want to leave this great place? Our program was definitely in good shape. We had beautiful facilities and Hunterdon County, New Jersey, was and still is a beautiful place. Well, one Sunday morning following my normal procedure of reading the Star Ledger Educational page, there was a job opening that really caught my attention.

EIGHT

After reading about the job opportunity at Elizabeth High School, I decided I had to apply in the hope I would just get an interview. I wanted to find out why so many people were saying, "forget about it." Forget about it being one of the best opportunities. The rumors were flying that it was the "best" job in the country.

After sending in my application I was offered a preliminary interview with the assistant superintendent, Frank Cicarell. Frank's responsibilities were athletics, physical education and physical welfare throughout the city of Elizabeth. To give you a feel of how big the school system was—there were 4,500 plus or minus students in grades ten thru twelve with a freshman house of 2,000 plus students. Along with this, there was a technical high school of 1,200 students. What a pool of potential athletes to pull from!

Frank, who worked his way up the power ladder from head football coach to principal to assistant superintendent and was one of the most respected men in town with very positive political ties, convinced the Board of Education, Mayor, and Superintendent that a top-notch athletic program should be given strong priority. He wanted to improve the atmosphere and discipline in the high school and felt that a good athletic program and its many support groups would help achieve this major goal.

Elizabeth was the last public school system in New Jersey that had its female population attend high school in its own building on a separate campus from the male facility.

After Title IX, the city built a state-of-the-art high school campus which housed a record number of students. They also refurbished the Jefferson Campus which was the male high school prior to this merger along with the Battin Campus which was the female campus. Property taxes in New Jersey financed its public school system, and Elizabeth with its many rateables had a large financial war chest.

After my initial interview I realized why it was advertised as such a special opportunity. I really felt that the support on all levels was going to be there including the Mayor, Board of Education and administration.

Before I knew it, things got interesting. I was invited back for round two of the interviewing process. During this interview a committee comprised of a person from those three areas along with Mr. Cicarell and myself, discussed what goals they expected and how we would accomplish them. They asked me what I would need to achieve their main goal of the football team becoming a nationally recognized program. After a pause, I started to tell them my method.

First, I would need a staff of quality coaches. I was told I would get the opportunity to interview existing staff members, and would not be pressured to keep anyone who coached the prior year. If I needed to bring in any coaches, I would have an opportunity to do so. In a district as large as Elizabeth there were always openings and if there were no teaching openings, they would create positions if necessary to get the right people in place.

At the time of the interview, they had a three tier concept: a varsity team, a junior varsity team and two freshman teams. After a discussion I told them that I favored a five tier system which would include a seventh and eighth grade team, a freshman team, a sophomore team, a junior varsity and finally our varsity. I explained to them I would need fifteen assistant coaches to organize a program this size along with a full time equipment manager and a full time athletic trainer.

Now the plot thickened. I was told as the head coach I would not have any classroom responsibility. My in-season responsibility would solely be that of being the head football coach. During the offseason they wanted me to set up an academic monitoring system for all of our athletes and help with security at our winter and spring athletic events in The Dunn Sports Center, a facility that could seat over 5,000 spectators. The added offseason responsibility was a real plus because now I was in contact with all athletes, not just the football players.

So the opportunity to recruit some great athletes who weren't playing football was going to be right there. There were some extremely talented basketball players and track kids who weren't playing football yet.

After hearing this, I took a shot and went for the gusto. I told them I also needed my top four assistants to have limited or no classroom responsibilities. The committee agreed and as things worked out three of my assistants had non-teaching responsibilities and were assigned to school security with the last hour of the school day during the season assigned to getting ready for football. My top assistant would be assigned to our state-of-the-art weight room next to my office.

My office was large enough to seat twenty plus students. Collectively, we came up with the idea that our football players would be assigned to me during their study hall and physical education class. We used their time to have a structured academic study hall system and a structured weight training program.

The next thing we discussed was equipment and they promised I would have an open checkbook to get nothing but the best. I was told I would get the opportunity to see what they had and I would be able to purchase what else I felt was needed. After about two and a half hours of discussion, we broke for lunch.

After lunch, we toured the facilities. The Dunn Sports Complex had enough floor space where I could have a seventy yard by fifty-three yard football field with a fifteen yard perimeter around it. It was amazing. I could have a complete indoor practice facility if I chose to do so.

The stadium and locker room were first class. It was like a small college facility with two and a half football fields to practice on. As I mentioned earlier, the weight room in the high school was second to none in the state, including Rutgers University at the time.

All that was needed were players and a school the size of Elizabeth. The potential was there and all you had to do was get them to come out and be accountable. Mr. Cicarell knew my two prior head coaching positions were at two suburban schools that had few minority athletes. He questioned me about this and I know he liked my answer. I told him "same problems, just different reasons." Also he got a good laugh when I said some of my coaching philosophies would have to be adjusted to utilize all the speed that would be available to me.

After this second interview things started to really get serious. The next time we got together we would discuss salary and how soon I could get released from my contractual obligations at North. Mr. Cicarell was going to call me to set up this appointment within a week. Needless to say the next few days I didn't sleep very well.

I had a tough time at North that week. We had a great returning nucleus and the kids were on target to get back to the big game the coming season. I felt guilty even thinking about the possibility of leaving North. It was time to talk to Bob Hopek because I knew they were going to contact him if I decided to take my third interview.

I set up an appointment to meet with Bob and finally told him I might be offered a job at another school. We spent the rest of the afternoon discussing why I should stay at North and reminisced about all the good times we had and how much fun was ahead of us. We discussed some of our favorite memories during our journey getting the program to where it was. Bob reminisced about his favorites, like the time we decided to have a professional wrestling fundraiser.

At that time, Gorilla Monsoon was the top gun in professional wrestling. He would come into large arenas that could seat at least 1,200 plus spectators and put on a show. He would split the gate profits seventy/thirty with you for allowing him to do so, seventy for him and thirty for you. The night we did this we packed the house with a standing room only crowd of close to 1,500 people at a ticket cost of ten dollars for general admission to twenty-five dollars ringside.

At the end of a great night we were counting the money in the athletic house while enjoying some beer and pizza. When we were done counting, I asked the Gorilla if he wanted to flip a coin for ten percent. Though Bob was nervous, he went along with the idea because if we lost and just got twenty percent we would still make $1,500 more than we expected. We called heads and we won, so the split went sixty-forty, and we wound up making about $8,000 for our efforts. It was like hitting the lottery.

Another favorite memory of Bob's was the time we were playing an undefeated South Hunterdon football team whose mascot was the eagle.

To have some fun at the end of our Friday practice, I asked the woodshop to make an eagle replica out of wood which I was going to split with my forehead after a fiery talk. My friend who was the shop teacher was supposed to run the grain of the wood north and south so it would be easy to break, but jokingly he ran it east and west. When I went to split the eagle in half, the only thing I split was my forehead. The kids were in a state of shock, but Hopek and the shop teacher were up on the hill watching this exhibition of stupidity dying laughing. Thank God we won the game. To this day I look at the scar on my forehead and remember that moment.

Then Bob and I got serious after these light moments and talked about some of our great victories over the last four years against some of the best Group III and Group IV programs in the state.

After this discussion with Bob, I realized how difficult it would be to leave North and especially how hard it would be to explain all this to our rising seniors. This was a class that I had grown very attached to. To say the least, my emotions were mixed and I was more confused now than before I went into Bob's office.

North was a great situation. Everything was in place—a returning group of players potentially as good as the state championship team, a very positive administration and support groups, a faculty that was tremendous and the envy of the state. Because of salary guide and teaching environment and facilities, they were as good as any in the state. Or do I accept the challenge that Elizabeth had to offer?

The next few days passed very slowly and I didn't think I was getting the call. They were calling back the final two for one more bout and it was already lunch time of the third day, the day they were to call. That afternoon I got the call and they told me to be there the next afternoon. I was one of the final two, the other being one of the most respected head coaches in North Jersey.

On the ride home that day I became very nervous and confused. My wife convinced me that night to stop being a baby, to just go to the interview with a positive frame of mind. She said that I had a win-win situation . . . stay at North or move on to Elizabeth. It was like making a fourth and one call but if the one you called didn't work, you had another chance to call a different one knowing it would work.

The final interview went great. We discussed and finalized my job description. What an opportunity. Initially, they wanted me to be the athletic director and head football coach. I told them I would rather be the assistant athletic director and head football coach with no classroom responsibility with my major responsibility being to build a state and nationally recognized football program. Now it was time to discuss salary.

In New Jersey your salary is based upon years of service and what degree you hold. At the time I didn't realize school districts had the option to start you anywhere they chose to on their salary guide. Their financial package was based on the top of the guide, something you didn't reach until you taught fourteen years in the district with a masters plus thirty degree. Also, the contract was a twelve-month contract and they allowed me to transfer my sick days from North. Unbelievable!

This package was twice what I was making at North, one of the state's best paying districts. Wow! No more side construction jobs needed to support my family. No more working summers painting houses or building patios, then showering and running a summer weight and conditioning program without compensation. It was football 365 days a year. It was like a college job without traveling. That was it. The interview was over and they said a decision would be made the next day and both finalists would be called with the results.

That morning I was called by Mr. Cicarell's office and I was told I was to be at the board of education office that evening to be introduced as the next head football coach at Elizabeth, a city rich in its athletic tradition of the forties, fifties and sixties but in the seventies there was a distinct drop off and it would be my job to regain its reputation.

I left school early to go over this decision with my wife. Initially, I decided not to accept the position, but then my loving wife, who knows me best, called me a chicken. She asked me, "What, are you afraid to coach against the state's best teams and coaches?" That was it. I decided to take it on and went to the meeting. I formally accepted the job, but asked them not to release it to the press for one day which would give me the opportunity to tell my players at North formally instead of them reading it in the papers.

Now I had to walk into the gymnasium and tell approximately ninety North Hunterdon football players who were returning for the '79 season and who bought into a concept based on loyalty to each other and our football program. These weren't only players who I had the luxury of being their head football coach, but kids who I went fishing with and jumped off the train trestle bridge into the river with—members of beautiful families whom I ate dinners with—it was very difficult. After the meeting was over, as they walked out some of the rising seniors called me "quitter" for leaving them prior to their senior season. It was difficult dealing with it. But there was no second guessing my decision.

The administration at North was great. They wished me well and allowed me to immediately break my contract. So off I went to Elizabeth that day—leaving the security of tenure for the second time, thinking about my first meeting of the players and how I should "act."

NINE

There I went with my plaid pants and shorts right out of the suburbs to the city, into the biggest high school in the country.

At North Hunterdon, my fastest player ran just under 4.7 for the forty-yard dash. In Elizabeth, kids were running 4.6 in street clothes and shoes. Speed—Speed—Speed! It was everywhere.

As Bob Toresco, my top assistant coach, and I were driving to work our first day, a new song came on the radio. It was titled, "Ain't No Stoppin' Us Now." I loved it and used it as the foundation of my first talk to the returning lettermen and rising underclassmen from the 1978 season.

My mind was speeding but under control, so many things to do again and the clock was ticking—more so than ever before. I came to the realization that my biggest enemy was that clock. Everything else I would and must control, with the unflappable support I was going to have from all involved. It gave me the patience and confidence that I knew I must have.

The principal, Dominic Parisi, was a "great man." He was "the Boss." He was my "Godfather" and made sure everything I was promised came to fruition because he was in charge and ran his building accordingly. He had to approve everything that went on there, from the hiring to the firing and everything in between. During my tenure at Elizabeth, he never refused one thing that I asked of him. He had his methods in this very political city. He was respected by both political parties. He knew how to work both sides.

Like I did many times, it was time to come up with a plan. I really pulled on my past experiences. I broke our major goal of becoming the program we all envisioned into smaller bites.

I.   Staffing—Must surround myself with winners
II. Player Participation
     A. Identify the athletes
     B. Make sure they stay eligible both academically and socially
III. Obtain the support of faculty and support groups
IV. Go over our athletic inventory and decide what additional equipment or uniforms I would need.
V.   Develop a playbook utilizing the talent and skills that were available—and boy, was talent available. All we had to do was get them out and keep them academically and socially eligible.

Well, taking one piece at a time, the first piece I addressed was developing a first class staff which took us two years to put together. My top three coaches were with the program from my first day along with four coaches who were there from the previous regime. Bob Toresco, who came with me from North Hunterdon, was a three-year starter at the University of Delaware under Tubby Raymond. Bob captained the team his senior year and played offensive guard. He was extremely knowledgeable. The University of Delaware offensive coaching philosophy of the forties, fifties, sixties and seventies was, and still is, one of the most intelligent concepts I ever studied. It is organized, disciplined and it gave you unlimited options to utilize the various talents your players have.

The second coach who came with me was Bill Nagy. Bill was a Bloomsburg University graduate and was a consummate defensive line coach who had professional playing experience. He was a great motivator and was a lot of fun to be around. Our kids loved him from the start. Kirk Hamrah was the third coach. He was our secondary and quarterback coach. Kirk played for Dunellen when I was coaching there and went to Colorado State. After a coaching change his freshman season, he transferred to Tarkio College where he was a starter for the next three years. By the way, Kirk was the student I locked in the closet that hot June day at Dunellen High School who went on and had a good college career.

Bob was assigned to the weight room permanently and organized and ran our in-season and out-of-season strength program. He was well-versed and respected, and spoke at many state and national clinics on this subject. Kirk and Bill were assigned directly to Mr. Parisi. They had no classroom responsibility. Their main purpose was discipline in the halls. All three coaches had release time during the day and at the end of the day, so that collectively we could spend time working on our program. Now that I had my top assistants in place, it was time to interview the existing staff. There were some quality coaches on that staff and three remained in the program all four years. The other slots were filled with new teacher/coaches who were hired by the district.

There were two other head coaches at Elizabeth who were given a great opportunity to build a state and nationally respected program. One was the head track coach and the other was the head basketball coach. Both were excellent and from the first time I met them I decided I had to convince them both to coach football on our staff, even though they had no experience coaching football.

Dave Costello, who was our indoor and outdoor head track coach, came aboard after our second season and was in charge of our speed development program. His brother, Frank Costello, was the head track coach at Maryland and also coached for the US Olympic team. He was a great source of information for us.

What a job Dave did for our football program. It was a beautiful thing how our athletes went from one sport to the other. We had twelve guys on our football roster who were both individual and team state champs in track along with being part of our '81 state championship program.

The final piece of the coaching puzzle was to convince Ben Candelino to become a member of our staff. Ben was our basketball coach who after the '79-80 school year was hired to build a championship program in basketball. After many conversations, I finally convinced him to coach football. Ben never coached football before, but I knew his help would be priceless.

We utilized his knowledge regarding man-to-man and zone play along with the pick and roll concept of offense and how you defend it when we taught our passing game and secondary play. We started integrating the basketball players into our program and the football players into the basketball program. Again our philosophy of one program should not improve at the cost of another program's success was not just lip service. As I repeated so many times, the best off-season program was to play another sport.

As we were putting our staff together we were constantly recruiting. And we were constantly monitoring development. Early on, once the word got out about our goals and how we were going to get there along with what would happen when we arrived, it was like we were giving away TVs. Before we knew it, there were 200 plus athletes wanting to be a part of our program. With this number of candidates, we could work toward excellence with a year-round commitment. Just like we did at prior schools, we had an in-season and out-of-season study hall system along with a strength and speed program for our athletes who didn't participate in a winter and/or spring sport.

Mr. Parisi loved this concept and our football athletes were assigned to me during their physical education class and study hall. We used this time to tutor them athletically, academically and socially. This was an immeasurable advantage. There definitely weren't too many high schools in the country that had this luxury.

We constantly monitored their progress throughout the school day. Our athletes carried around attendance and progress reports that they had to get initialed, every class, every day for some, and some were weekly. Any problems were corrected immediately, from not being able to practice to where if it continued without improvement, you would be suspended from the team. No deviations from the rules were permitted.

At the end of our 1981-82 season, we had 250 players in our five-tier program attached to this concept. One of our proudest accomplishments that championship year was that eighty-five percent of our varsity players were on the principal's honor roll. Twenty-five of that number were on the high honor roll. We really stuck to the concept of scholar/athlete. This was a lesson I learned at a very young age when my father had to adjust my attitude toward school work.

Ninety percent of our faculty bought into our academic monitoring program even though at times it meant they had to do a little extra bookkeeping work. The rest weren't up for the new concept. But Mr. Parisi had his methods to convince certain faculty members that this program had his blessing and they had to conform.

I remember distinctly the first spring at Elizabeth. Our journey toward the Meadowlands and the state championship had just begun. A college coach came into our state-of-the-art weight room and was looking at a giant chart that we kept right by the entrance way. On it we didn't list how strong or how fast you were. We listed each player's grades and record of his class attendance. At the end of each marking period, if there was no improvement your chances of moving up the depth chart were affected. We rewarded positive class performance with various perks. In the seventies and eighties there were no rules regarding selling candy and soda in the building during the school day. We struck a deal with the local soda and candy distributors. We installed ten soda machines and housed two candy stores within the building.

We used our athletes who were in good standing to work in the stores and also keep our machines filled. These two areas would generate $2,000 of revenue a week which we shared with other programs. Along with our other fundraisers we would raise approximately $80,000 per school year. We used this money to reward positive performance. It was great during and at the end of each marking period. Good test scores and grades were financially rewarded. I did like my father did to me-so much for an A or B, C was exactly what it was—average, so all you got was a pat on the back. D's and F's weren't tolerated. Not only were there financial rewards, but we dressed our athletes in some great athletic wear. Shoes, jackets, hats, and sweats were all earned by our players who participated and believed in our concept.

One of the most enjoyable things we would do was we would have our position coaches take our players out to some of the finest restaurants in the metropolitan area. We would also have a guest faculty member or two invited to go along. It was a beautiful sight seeing our kids all dressed up, sitting in these fine restaurants, behaving like gentlemen, dining on things they never had before while interacting with their peers, teachers and coaches. How do you keep a straight face at times? I remember one day when one of my players came back from a night out. They went over to Staten Island to an all-you-could-eat steak, ribs and shrimp place; ten players, two coaches and one faculty member. Well, I saw him at breakfast and I asked him, "How were things?" He said, "Everything was delicious, but the shrimp were crunchy." He said, "Coach, I put the red sauce on like you said to do, but they were really crunchy." I then asked, "Did you take the shell off?" He looked at me with his great smile and said, "Was I supposed to?" These special moments I counted as victories when defining winning.

After a staff meeting, followed by a meeting with our rising 1981 seniors, we came up with a tee-shirt logo that would be used for one of the big fundraisers; one in which we would award our football donors with a tee-shirt.

Our mascot was a minuteman similar to the Boston Patriot mascot. So we made a logo with the minuteman pointing a finger at whoever is reading the tee-shirt with the statement under him in bold print—"See Ya In the Meadowlands." On the back of the t-shirt was an outline of the state of New Jersey with two stars in it, one where Elizabeth was and the other where the Meadowlands was—better known as Giant Stadium, the home of the state playoffs.

We had 600 shirts made up for the fundraiser and another 600 to sell. They were gone in a month. It seemed like everyone in town had one. What we were doing was telling everyone that we would measure the success of this season solely on making it to the "big game."

We knew in order to just play for the state championship we would have to beat at least three of the four state's top programs during our regular season schedule.

Other things we did with the money from the fundraiser was to reimburse the board athletic fund. This money was used to supplement the cost of our breakfast, lunch and supper programs. We made sure our athletes were eating three meals a day. We would also take our tenth thru twelfth grade athletes away to camp for a week prior to the beginning of school. We also would have catered coaching staff meetings. We would pay for our athletes to visit colleges, if the college they were visiting didn't do so. And we would make sure all who visited colleges, looked and acted the part of an Elizabeth High School football player. We would bring our athletes to summer performance camps and at the beginning of each month we would make a nice contribution to a program that Mr. Parisi had to help the less fortunate students.

After our second season, we were playing 500 plus ball on the field, but we were really winning in a big way in other areas. Our participation in the program was way up and our behavior in the school and community was very good.

Our staff was in place. Our equipment and facilities were in great shape. We wanted for nothing. It was time to make a statement.

TEN

Our first big win in 1981 came against Westfield High School, which, at the time, was the number one team in the state and was coached by one of the winningest coaches in New Jersey history, the legendary Coach Gary Kehler, who for the first two years wasn't happy about his margin of victory over us. Westfield was heavily favored and just got by. That just wasn't good enough for him.

The past year, they scored a field goal late in the fourth quarter for the game's only points. After the kickoff, we could not move the ball, so we punted back to them with a minute plus left to play, thinking they would let the clock run out. They chose to use two timeouts to try to score just for the sake of putting more points on the board. That didn't set well with me. I really let my temper go at the end of the game, and Coach Kehler knew exactly where I was coming from and how we as a team felt about it.

Our game preparation for this third meeting between us and Westfield was flawless and our game plan was in place, but more importantly, we carried it out and beat them in every aspect of the game. I believe it was the largest margin of defeat in his coaching career to that date. We really had fun with it. We got the ball back for our last possession on offense at our own twenty yard line with four minutes to go, up by four scores. We decided we were going to run the clock out by just pounding them from tackle to tackle.

Before you knew it, the ball was in the red zone and we were going in. Everyone was yelling, "Use your timeouts and score another one." Now it was first and goal, and we had two timeouts with a minute to play. I finally called timeout and walked out to the field slow, got my kids in the huddle and told them that when play resumed we would hit a knee and then call timeout again. After our second timeout I told the kids, "Get in a sharp huddle, break and sprint to the line of scrimmage and hit a knee again," this time letting the clock run out. Westfield got the message loud and clear.

We were now ranked in the top ten by the state newspaper. But next we were playing Union, the returning state champs, who had two of the state's top college recruits on their starting offensive team along with a great supporting class of returning lettermen. They were the team to beat and we had to beat them somewhere during a championship run.

Our kids' confidence level wasn't there yet and we lost a very tough game to Union 19-14. In the locker room at halftime, I remember the looks on their faces. They just felt we were a little out-manned. We knew we were good, but felt they were a little better. This attitude sure changed the next time we got a shot at them.

After that tough defeat, we rattled off six straight victories and again moved into the state's top ten ranking. Along the way we beat three more state ranked programs.

It was now time for the playoffs and because of strength of schedule and power points we were the top seed and all four teams in our bracket were ranked in the top ten, with Union and Westfield ranked in the top five. During the season after our victory over Westfield, they didn't lose another game and their victory over Union was Union's only defeat.

Finally our tee-shirt logo of "See Ya in the Meadowlands" was going to be a reality. That Sunday night when the play-off seedings came out, we were number one. Westfield and Union were two and three respectively and Barringer, the best program in Newark at the time, was seeded number four.

Every year the top seeded teams in our section got to play both games in the Meadowlands. I was having my Sunday night meal of spaghetti and meatballs at my mother's house after a very long day of coaching staff meetings which started at six a.m., when the world stopped!

For whatever reason, they put the Westfield vs. Union semi-final in the Meadowlands and we were told that our game would be at our home field. No way! After a couple glasses of my family wine and a little coaxing from my family, I started calling everyone. The Mayor of Elizabeth, Mr. Parisi, Mr. Cicarell, Mr. Gold, who was the Board President, and finally the Mayor of Newark and the very connected head football coach at Barringer High School. I was letting everyone know that we would not accept second billing. We had earned the right to top billing. Anything less would not be acceptable. We worked too hard on our road, our mission to play in Giant Stadium and no one was going to change what was right.

I was told late that night by the state's paper that a special meeting was going to take place early Monday morning to discuss my concerns by the state athletic association. Well, I guess the pressure of the state's most powerful mayors was just too much to handle. Mr. Parisi told me Sunday night to get in touch with our varsity players and coaches, have them dressed in game day attire and report to the main auditorium at nine-thirty a.m. where he would hold a press conference.

Finally at nine-fifteen a.m., we received the phone call from the state athletic association. We were in. Mr. Parisi allowed my varsity coaching staff to have an in-service day that Monday. We spent the day continuing to work on the game plan and the coming week's itinerary, counting for every minute. Talk about being organized.

My job was to be the orchestra leader. I had to make sure everyone knew the music perfectly. Not everyone wants to be a boss. But if you choose that role and take on that responsibility, shame on you if you don't lead. I had a great inner circle of very loyal assistants, administrators, teachers, custodians and friends who for the next two weeks, as they did all year, rallied and helped every way they could.

The theme of our game plan was to take advantage of certain situations that we had control over. The number one thing that we had that our opponents didn't have was such strong support from our administration who would do anything I asked as long as we did it in the best interest of our student athletes.

Mr. Parisi worked out the school day for us so we had early dismissal all week for our players and coaches. Preparing to play on the Astroturf, we used our connection to practice at Montclair State University. We practiced on their Astroturf Wednesday, followed by a practice at the Meadowlands on Thursday. Our Board of Education on Tuesday located sixty pairs of Astroturf shoes from a major distributor and had them over-nighted to us so we had them for Wednesday practice and the game on Sunday. The other teams used shoes that were on hand courtesy of the Jets and Giants.

What a great practice we had at Montclair State. We got all our heavy stuff done—tackle to tackle offense, goal line. Then we practiced control thud defense. Coach Burns, the Head Coach at Rutgers, said it was one of the best organized high school practices he'd ever seen. You have to be a real disciplined team to run this drill properly and that day we were doing our best to get better.

On Thursday, we got to practice for 105 minutes on the field in the Meadowlands and we got to use the locker room for forty-five minutes.

After arriving we went over everything we would do game day. Then on to the field. For the first twenty minutes of our practice, I let them have fun and do what they wanted to do their first time on the big stage. It was great to watch eighty-five people having such an enjoyable and memorable moment together. It was like allowing a bunch of kids to open their Christmas presents together and getting everything they dreamed of. They were taking pictures and running around, just enjoying the moment.

The last eighty-five minutes of practice we got to work in a very serious manner. It reminded me of an orchestra at Carnegie Hall getting ready for a beautiful performance. Everyone worked together with only one thing in mind—team harmony—with maximum effort.

The week ended that Sunday night with a beautifully executed game plan. We won by five touchdowns and shut the Barringer High School offense completely down. Earlier in the day, Union beat up on Westfield so we knew we were going to get another shot at Union, this time for the "state championship." We didn't think much about our Barringer victory. We had Union on our mind.

After our victory on Sunday night, we really only had two days to get ready for our Thanksgiving game against a lower-ranked team. We definitely did not want a letdown. We kept our intensity, but we had a different delivery in our approach to this Thanksgiving Day game. We kept emotion out of it.

We were very businesslike and practiced with the concept that we were going to use all of our sixty players who were going to dress for that game.

We won the game against Cranford going away and after the first series of the second half neither the first or second team played the remainder of the game. Our younger players got a chance to be on the field and did a great job finishing off the victory.

We gave our kids Friday and Saturday off. During our staff meetings over the next two days, we were interrupted a few times by our players stopping by. But we shooed them away and got back to business preparing for Union. Again from our Sunday night team meeting to kick-off, everything was down to the minute exactly how it was going to be done. We made sure there was no wasted energy. Everything we did had to have a purpose.

ELEVEN

After a film breakdown of sixteen games of Union's offense, defense and kicking game, we finally felt we had a grip on their coaching concepts. Of course we knew the physical matchups from playing them earlier in the year, but we felt through our growth during the season we were now ready. We also acknowledged that our schedule of teams that we played was stronger and that was what gave us the power points to be seeded number one. We used all the information we had available, and boy did we have a lot, to come up with our plan for victory.

Now it was time to institute the plan. We all had to communicate and understand what the plan was and what everybody's role was to be. Sunday afternoon we had a wonderful brunch set up for our players. Already the attitude of quiet humility was developing. After eating, we had position meetings to discuss all aspects of their assignments and how their assignment affected the big picture.

Our support people including our walking boss, who was a man from town who kept the players in check, my father, our public relations people and even "God" knew what the itinerary was and what their roles consisted of. Everyone was on the "clock." A little note about "God," for surely this was not done out of disrespect. Every week we prayed as a team with different guest prayer leaders from the city's churches before and after the games. After our loss to Union, game three of the season, the following game this elderly, gray-haired gentleman, showed up on the sidelines before the game.

We allowed no one on our sidelines unless they had a part in our game plan. No part. You're a spectator. Watch from the bleachers and be one of now 10,000 people who filled our stands. What great 50/50's we ran with the band parents. Our football fund's share was at least $3,000 per home game.

Well, getting back to "God"—I walked over to the elderly guy during warmups and asked who he was. He told me his name and that he had played for Elizabeth forty-five years ago. I said that's nice and was just about to call security when he smiled and said, "I just want to be near the action." I broke down. I called security over and told them to give him a sideline pass.

All of our kids and coaches noticed him when we came off the field. How could you not notice this beautiful elderly man with white hair dressed in our game colors, cheering as we went by?

In my pregame talk, I touched on the subject that God wants us to have confidence and to love and believe in self, and to reinforce that belief, He is on our sidelines today.

It was great. Everyone on our sidelines was dressed in black or white and there he was, our new confidence builder, dressed in a beautiful red sweater standing in a position of honor. It was very emotional to say the least. That day with confidence and belief in self and neighbor we started our streak of eight big wins.

Back to game preparation. Once our position meetings concluded, we had a thirty minute lifting session followed by a thirty minute agility stations drill. After they all showered, we had soup and sandwiches and made sure everyone got home safely.

Monday was a normal school day for everyone. After a study hall session, we stretched out and had a walk through by position, by team.

We followed this with a team meeting and film session and then they enjoyed a team meal after we were done.

Tuesday was a half day at school for the coaches and players. We had lunch on the road at a nice restaurant in Montclair and then practiced for two hours on the Astroturf at Montclair State University. After practice, we traveled in our beautiful, leased black cruisers back to Elizabeth where we ate dinner as a team.

Wednesday was a normal school day followed by practice. At practice, we emphasized position by position how we were going to attack the Union system. Not emphasizing personnel—our kids knew the personnel and were licking their chops at getting another shot, so there was no need for us to mention players' names. They knew who they were playing against. According to the newspapers, we were getting the "opportunity" to play against a much publicized Union High School, one of the premier programs in the state and country.

We emphasized during practice that we must stay humble until kickoff.

Thursday was a half day at school. We had lunch as a team with our school administrators. Our captains thanked them for their wonderful support in helping us get to where we were and promised them we would arrive at the next station soon.

We drove to the Meadowlands, did what we had to do with no fanfare. We practiced for ninety minutes. It was an extremely disciplined businesslike practice. After practice was over, we got on our buses and went home to Elizabeth for a warm team meal.

Friday was a normal school day followed by a light practice. We emphasized that this was a dress rehearsal for Saturday.

Talk about getting to the edge. We were prepared and ready. Like a fine violin player tuning his instrument, you just knew when everything was ready.

Gameday, we knew what time Union was going to arrive. We were told to arrive ten minutes after they did. We made up our mind to be fashionably late.

We boarded our black Greyhound cruisers and drove north on the Jersey Turnpike from the famous Exit 13A three exits north to the Meadowlands. The music was great on the bus. "Get Down on It," "Ain't No Stoppin' Us Now," "Planet Patrol," and a couple of hard rock songs for our North end boys. Everybody just relaxed and enjoyed "The Ride." Two of my assistants went to the Meadowlands early to set up two six foot speakers near the entrance of our locker room. The buses drove right into the stadium and dropped us off about fifty paces from the locker room, just a long enough walk for one song to play. We got off the bus, serious business, with our seniors carrying the memory of the rope.

The rope was something we gave our seniors at camp. We cut it into pieces that our seniors carried with them all year. Before boarding the bus, Kirk Hamrah had the seniors burn this rope and used the ash to emphasize the bond the seniors would have the remainder of their lives.

Talk about getting peoples' attention. The Union players who were standing around their locker room definitely sensed the atmosphere and couldn't help hearing the bass of our entrance song "Planet Patrol."

We emphasized no emotion until kickoff. Warmups were crisp and we kept them as quiet as possible. All you heard was the game, the sound of punts, the sound of breaking a huddle, the sound of our defensive leaders barking out signals. What a great atmosphere. Finally we went back into the locker room for the last time, to an atmosphere that only a few of us have been blessed to feel, a strong feeling of confidence in each other and in a plan that we all understood and believed in.

Finally—game time.

We executed flawlessly on offense, defense, and kicking game. Our sideline control was poetry in motion.

On offense, we ran the ball extremely well using their defensive alignment and secondary concepts to our benefit. We took advantage of their size and aggressiveness with a great trapping scheme. We attacked their man to man pass coverage with play action and speed. We controlled the ball and the game with an offensive team that had fifteen Division I or IA scholarship athletes who attended and graduated from schools such as Princeton, University of Massachusetts, Virginia, Lehigh, Purdue and Northern Utah to name a few. Our leading rusher,

Rodney Carter, an All-American at Purdue who played four years in the NFL, was an example of someone who always gave such great effort, and was one of the many examples of what the Class of 1982 was all about. That class to this day was and still is what the commitment of the 1981 football team was all about. Every one of those young men continued after high school being champions in their lives.

Defensively, we had an "offensive" frame of mind. We attacked their high powered Wing-T concept. We made up our mind we were going to play on their side of the line of scrimmage.

We had a 350 pound nose tackle who benched 400 pounds and was unblockable. He powered his way to gap control and caused havoc in their backfield. We used him as a substitute for our starting nose tackle, Willie Wooten. Willie was a back-up fullback who was five feet, ten inches tall, 185 lbs. and ran the forty in 4.4. He was about as tough as you could get and was the best dancer in the school. Willie, because of his speed, led our team in tackles behind the line of scrimmage. We started Willie every play from a different position. What a game he had. That one film helped him earn a full football scholarship to Delaware State.

Our three linebackers, who received scholarships to Virginia, Purdue, and Arizona Western, along with our corners, who played at Nebraska and Lehigh, and our safeties, who played at Delaware State, along with our four top subs, all played college football while receiving full football scholarships. All were having a party around the football with great gang tackling. They gave the number one team in the state a big goose egg on the scoreboard in a definitely overpowering manner: Elizabeth 21—Union 0.

What I was most proud of was the manner in which this team carried themselves during the championship week and the remainder of the 81-82 school year both on and off the field, in the classroom and with their personal lives.

They were an extremely humble group who realized there was always room for improvement. All you had to do was work hard and believe in yourself and your teammates, and you could achieve a goal. Our goal was winning, and we did so fair and square as both students and athletes. At our awards day, when we gave our team their state championship rings and jackets, I emphasized to them about not letting this be their last accomplishment, but continue on with this championship attitude. They sure were and still are a special group of men who I'll always love and remember.

TWELVE

I loved my staff at Elizabeth. I was blessed with a lot of good people who would work endless hours to give everyone on the team their maximum effort. There was a personality for everyone. We were all very different, but our efforts were equal and our direction was the same. But in education sometimes it's hard to keep good people around. Within a year's time, two of my top assistants decided to leave education and go into the business world. Bob Toresco wanted a shot at being a head coach, but was finding it hard to find anything better than he had at Elizabeth.

I was offered some really good jobs over the next year and one really interested me even though down deep inside the only job I wanted was a job at Rutgers University. Out of the blue in January, 1983, I talked with Dr. Hall who I had the pleasure to work for when he was the superintendent of schools for the North Hunterdon School District.

He was the superintendent of a district that was in political turmoil because of a very divisive strike which resulted in some union members spending a night or two in jail for their participation in the strike. The union leader was a very powerful leader. She and the administration and the board of education weren't on the best of terms and were at odds about a lot of things. No disrespect intended, but I remember a quote from Mark Twain, "God practiced making fools until He perfected his technique. Then He created school boards." This is not entirely true. I have dealt with some great board members. I'd better say this since my brother and sister were board members in my hometown. The overall morale in Dr. Hall's district and schools was being affected by this constant battle. The athletic program, especially football, fell upon tough times and had losing seasons over a five year stretch. This added to the already poor morale.

The superintendent felt if he could return the football program to its glory days things would improve. After another losing season in '82, the head football coach resigned under pressure. There were two candidates in the district who applied for the position. One was the retired former football coach who coached some very good teams prior to this negative turn around. He was a tough guy who was his own man. The other candidate was an assistant coach who grew up in Matawan and was the favorite of the union president. The decision, or lack of a decision, to hire either of these coaches added to the district turmoil and divided the district even more.

Dr. Hall contacted me regarding the position of head football coach to see if I was interested. He told me he was going to create a non-teaching administrative position for me and my main concern would be to improve the football facilities and get the program and booster club back on track. He told me that their number one opponent was Brick Township, a nationally ranked program with its legendary coach who had the most wins of any person who coached high school football in New Jersey. This was a team that Matawan never beat. Dr. Hall felt that if Matawan could ever beat Brick, things would immediately improve. The financial package he offered was very flattering. Things became interesting, a chance to make a statement plus a good financial boost for my family.

I had a lot to think about. By now I realized what it took to win, strong support from community and administration along with a strong desire from faculty and students to work together to make things better. After spending a few days visiting the district, I felt the goal of building a winning program at Matawan was achievable even though the union leader would be tough to work with. I had confidence and so did Dr. Hall regarding my ability to win her over and get her on the same page with our concept of improving the atmosphere at Matawan both on and off the field.

I was a little naive and at the time did not realize what negative politics could do regarding achieving a goal. You had to have everyone pulling in the same direction with total focus on getting to the point everyone agreed upon. If you had someone of authority not on board, things became difficult and total success was hard to come by.

I made up my mind if the administrators at Elizabeth would give Bob, my top assistant, the head job I would strongly consider accepting the challenge at Matawan. After a few meetings with the Elizabeth administration there were some mixed emotions, but when they agreed with me regarding the position of head football coach at Elizabeth, I decided to accept the job at Matawan and resigned my position at Elizabeth.

My official appointment the next day at a special board meeting at Matawan was supposed to be just a press conference atmosphere. Little did I know that the union president was going to use it as a political platform and make things tough right from the start. The meeting was scheduled to last an hour followed by a dinner meeting with myself, the superintendent and his top administration along with the board to discuss my game plan and responsibilities. Well, it was close to midnight before the open board meeting came to an end. The union leaders did everything they could do to make it tough. But finally I was officially appointed to my new responsibilities.

Our dinner meeting turned into breakfast at the local diner. We discussed many things into the early hours of the morning, but the main topic was the athletic facilities and how we could go about making them better. The board administrator had quotes close to $250,000 to do what was necessary and he felt that this amount of money would be difficult to find in an already tight budget for the coming year. I said, "Give me a few days to come up with a plan and maybe I can get it accomplished for much less." One of the biggest complaints that the union had was the amount of money they were paying "this outsider" to come into their district and coach football. So I felt if I could get the facilities in order at a minimum cost to the district things would be forgotten and I would become an accepted member of the Matawan "fraternity."

Using my connections in construction along with some local contractors, I came up with a budget to achieve everything they wanted regarding the facilities at a $200,000 savings.

The board gave this plan their blessing and we started work. First we improved the field irrigation system, re-sodded the field, repaired and painted the press box along with the bleachers. All the material was donated or purchased at cost. We used the parents, coaches, players, and local community people as our labor force. It was great! We were developing a strong sense of pride along with esprit de corps. Our locker room area was also vastly improved with new lockers, new team room and a long overdue coach's office. When the construction was done, everything was painted in school colors. The place looked great. Everyone was excited and we were working together beautifully. That was everyone, but the union president. She never lightened up and was a constant thorn. Dr. Hall kept on saying to me, "If you could only beat Brick now. She would have to get on the bandwagon."

Well, I copied my prior scripts. I started putting a staff together, met with parents, teachers, and students. Anyone who wanted to be a part of the program, I found time for. The community was definitely getting excited.

I decided to hire the local favorite son of the union president who didn't get the head job and told him to be patient. Once we got things turned around, he would get his opportunity like my previous top assistants did. The staff was coming along nicely, but I still needed two more coaches on offense.

I was lucky to find Bob Davis, who was the back-up quarterback to Joe Namath with the Jets, between careers. Bob wanted to work with teenagers and coaches. The timing was perfect. I was told by the fall they would have a full time position for him so he made the commitment and accepted a part-time position until then. Little did I realize that Dr. Hall would have to go back on his promise regarding a full time position and Bob just coached that one season and did a great job.

There was only one teaching opening in the high school at the end of the '83 school year. An English teacher retired so I was told if I could find an English teacher with a coaching background he would have a leg up for the job. I posted the job in the state newspaper and had a handful of applicants. After an initial interview process my first choice was a guy named Charlie Weis who later on in his career became the head coach at Notre Dame. We came to an agreement about his responsibilities and what I expected from him once the job was his.

Now I had a full staff in place and as a staff we started working on our playbook, dissecting films and learning personnel.

Charlie came to our first two staff meetings late because of summer league softball. When he called me and told me he was going to be late for the next meeting, I told him to please leave his playbook in my mailbox and wished him luck. I then offered the position to my second choice who luckily did not have a job yet and he accepted the position immediately.

Brick was our second game. So we set up our practice schedule and game plan concept to beat them from day one. We didn't want to overlook our first game, but we felt we were a much better team than our first opponent and decided to go with this concept.

As a coach I remember the old school guys saying if it works keep on running it until someone stops it. This was my fourth head coaching job. Our goal was the same. Build a winning program and in order to do so you must beat your toughest opponents. Once the goal was in place the method was the same. Just outwork your opponents and use all of the information available to you to come up with a plan to do so.

My ears were always ringing with—"All you have to do is beat Brick, all you have to do is beat Brick and things would be great . . . All you gotta' do is win."

THIRTEEN

The fall of 1983 came quickly. The big question still loomed. Would this be the year that Matawan would finally beat Brick Township?

After all the work that we put in during the spring and summer on and off the field, improvements were recognizable. Our players were definitely buying in and the talent level was there. We had great success recruiting some athletes who did not play football the prior year. One of those candidates was a six foot, two and a half inch tall, 210 pound, rising senior who I picked out as a very good prospect when I went and watched the end of the year school play. Yes, the school play.

The play was "Oklahoma." I saw this young man who could sing, dance and had a great sense of showmanship and I visualized what he would look like in a football uniform. After a few meetings with him and his mother, he decided he would come out for football his senior year for the first time.

Gerry had such a great year that he was awarded a full football scholarship at Northeastern University along with making some post-season all area football teams.

Our pre-season went well and we beat our first opponent soundly. It was now time to play Brick. The game, if we could possibly win, would make everything better. Brick was ranked number one in the state after the first week and the papers were already saying that again they would be favorites to finish in that honored position. During the summer I found out everything I could locate about their program and its coach. I discovered a lot of interesting tendencies while watching fifteen years of films on them along with talking to coaches and people who knew about the program which was among the elite programs in the state, and its leader.

After all our research, we came up with both a psychological and strategical game plan. We based this game plan on the fact that their coach had been doing the same thing year in and year out on all levels from Pop Warner to the varsity because it had worked so well so why change it. I mean from wearing the same suit since he had been the head coach at Brick, to his methods of warm-up, to game strategies; he had done it the same. Why change or fix something that wasn't broken? There was a definite method to their madness, plus a little superstition surrounded the program.

I told our staff and players that it was a real plus for us to know what decisions he was going to make prior to the need to make such a decision, especially when Brick played at home. His pre-game ritual was something he had been doing for thirty plus years. My plan was to use all this information to our benefit and disrupt his pattern of victory.

Over the summer I visited their field about a half dozen times with him not knowing I was there. Game week I called their athletic director and asked if I could come over and check the facilities. He told me he would check with "Coach" to see when he was available. From all my homework I understood why Coach Wolf was such a powerful administrator, politician and football coach. But meeting him in person was a real trip. He definitely had a powerful personality and it was very obvious things were done his way.

In our meeting, I asked to see the locker rooms we would use prior to the game and at half time. We discussed security measures we should follow after the game and what was expected from us prior to the game. I stayed very quiet and was extremely humble in my mannerism always emphasizing the point of what a thrill it was going to be to coach against him. After our meeting, I left and was driving back to Matawan very excited because I truly believed our game plan had a chance. Our motto was, "Where there is confusion, there is gain."

Step one was to disrupt their organized pre-game sequences. We rented a crane with a cherry picker basket on it so our scouts would be the same height and have the same view as their scouts would have. The home coaching staff sat above the press box with a great view of the field from the fifty yard line. The visitors' coaching box was in the visitors' bleachers about sixty percent lower than the press box on the home side of the field. This was an unfair advantage especially when you're looking for alignments of both offensive and defensive sets.

Knowing that the athletic director would not make the decision okaying us to park the crane near our sidelines, we had to wait for "Coach" to come to the field to make that decision. Our first surprise was in progress.

I knew that Coach Wolf had every minute accounted for prior to when his team came out for warmups and taking ten minutes out of his so very organized schedule would be frustrating. I had the crane parked in the parking lot so when he arrived, BAM, it was right there. As soon as I saw him come out, I pounced on him like a linebacker pouncing on a fumble. In contrast to my first humble meeting with Coach Wolf, my second meeting was drastically different. I used my best "How You Doin" Italian routine and almost told him instead of asking him about what I planned on doing. I could see him start to unravel, but he did his best not to get upset and after some conversation which I tried to control, he agreed that it was okay to put the crane on our sidelines so our coaches would have a fair view of the field. I thanked him and reestablished the fact that it was only fair. You had to see the excitement in our locker room when our team heard step one was accomplished. The cherry picker was in place.

Step Two: We knew exactly what time they came out and we were told we should come out three minutes before them. We were purposely five minutes late and lined up at the wrong end of the field to disrupt them even more. When Brick came on the field there was total confusion. Again we won a small battle.

Step Three: While the Brick players were stretching, Coach Wolf would walk around and talk with them and give them gum. Knowing this, I walked over to him, put my arm around him like he was my long-lost brother and started talking to him like we were best friends. I apologized for going to the wrong end of the field and being late, but I could see he wanted nothing to do with me and was getting upset.

When we went into the locker room we emphasized Phase I was a success. It was now game time. We decided prior to the coin toss that if we won the toss we would defer to the second half knowing he would take the ball. Well, it worked. He chose to receive. We studied his alignment and saw if we kicked off from the left hash his left side would pull off their alignment quickly to set their wall up for a return. We decided to squib kick it left with our three fastest kids on the left side of the ball who would attack his players who were aligned on the left. Our best ball hawk would then go after the ball, followed by the kicker. We must have practiced this kick a hundred times during the pre-season and it worked to the letter. We recovered the ball and four plays later we were in the end zone running to the short side of the field, knowing their defense would over-align to the wide side. Quickly after the touchdown, we went for two points and before you knew it the score was 8-0. It was a beautiful thing and we wound up soundly defeating the number one team in the state. We pulled off what the newspapers called a "miracle" victory.

Our fans were in shock. No one believed we would pull it off except our team. There was no party though. That old saying about "there are as many people who want to see you lose as win" was doubly true that night in Matawan.

This big win made the union rep more determined than ever to make things difficult. Because of her strong desire to get her favorite "local son" the head coaching job, the superintendent was unable to keep promises that he made both financially and professionally. Her opinion of me as an outsider would never change no matter what accomplishments we made.

After a very good season which included qualifying for the state championship and having more W's than L's, I decided I would put all my eggs into one basket and go after a coaching job at Rutgers University, opening the opportunity for the "hometown boy" to get the head coaching job at Matawan. He'd inherit a program that was in great shape with a three-level program that would return twenty-five lettermen who would win the state championship the following year.

By now, more than ever before, I realized how important it was for everyone to be on the same page to achieve a goal.

Under pressure, the administrator at Matawan decided that he had to bend. It was hard for me to accept because I felt, and to this day still believe, if he had stayed strong with his promises we would have overcome the jealousy and negative attitude that the program was getting by a "small" minority. Sometimes you must step back for the overall good.

New game plan. It was time to go after something I really wanted to do. That was being a coach on the college level. There was going to be a possible opportunity at Rutgers, the State University, and I was going to do my best to convince anyone involved with Rutgers that I wanted to be a part of building upon Rutgers' great football tradition.

FOURTEEN

When the Rutgers administration decided to let Frank Burns go along with his great staff because they felt he wasn't the man to take them to the next level, it began a downward spiral that took twenty plus years to straighten out. Finally they decided to hire a "Jersey Guy," Coach Schiano, and the program is no longer the butt of a lot of jokes.

The administration hired Dick Anderson almost immediately after the '83 season. Dick was an assistant from Penn State and after he was appointed Rutgers head football coach, I was his first interview. Things went very well, plus I was getting great support from the press and felt I had a good chance at being offered an assistant coaching position. I knew Dick and the Penn State staff from working on their staff at Happy Valley for the past two years at their summer camp program for high school players.

Coach Anderson took six or seven weeks to decide which high school coach from "Jersey" he was going to make a part of his staff. My name and another successful coach from Central Jersey received a lot of press regarding which one of us would get the job.

Dick called me and said that the decision would be made prior to the national letter of intent day which was when the incoming freshman recruits had to decide what colleges they were going to play for.

A few days before that date, I received two very positive phone calls. One of those calls came from a Penn State assistant who recruited New Jersey. He jokingly said, "I guess we're going to be opponents the first weekend of football this year when Penn State lines up to play Rutgers." The other came from a Rutgers athletic administrator I knew, and he said he heard I was the choice. Wow, was I excited. Nothing was definite yet, but things looked awfully good.

The decision day finally came and so did the phone call. Coach was stuttering and having a difficult time. That's when I interrupted him and asked, "What's your decision?" He told me I wasn't his choice. My answer to him politely was, "You just made your first mistake." But I wished him luck.

There I was. No job. Remember, I left the job at Matawan for a lot of reasons and put all my eggs in one basket to go after the Rutgers position. The decision on what I was going to do next came fast.

I decided I would start up my maintenance business again. I put together a business plan like I was developing a game plan for my next opponent. As always, I had my wife's support. My family's confidence in my abilities and work ethics relaxed me during this time of transition yet again.

I purchased two trucks and hired employees like I was putting a football team together. Instead of recruiting athletes for various positions, I was hiring carpenters, roofers and laborers to fill my needs.

In order to be a successful coach, you must be able to sell. Instead of selling a coaching concept to my players, I was selling my new company's ability to problem solve. I designed our company around the ability to fulfill all forms of building maintenance needs.

In New Jersey, anyone could become a general contractor. All you needed was the ability to get the job, do the job, collect the check and make sure the check was good.

In the beginning, I sought out every contact I made during my fifteen years of high school coaching. Seventy percent of my thirty plus employees were either students I coached or taught or young men from my hometown whom I knew and more importantly, who knew me. I also used my contacts with players I coached to keep my team playing, oh, I mean working.

Bob Bartnett, who I had the pleasure to coach for three years, was both a football team player and a good man. When he found out what Coach was doing, he gave me enough business over the next half dozen years to help me keep my team working, all on a handshake. It sure felt good to have a business relationship built on trust; same foundation of everyone involved knowing what the goal was, having a game plan and the ability to pull it off.

This one contact with Bob and the company he worked for, United Land Resources, helped me not only financially, but also with a business education that was priceless. We did whatever was needed twenty-four/seven to help maintain four plus million square feet of commercial buildings. If I didn't know how to do what was needed to do, I found someone I knew to help me get it done.

Uniforms were always an important part of building a winning program. You had to look good and feel good about what you represented along with a catchy saying as a battle cry for what goals the team wanted to achieve.

My company logo was S.I.S., which stood for Specializing in Service. People would ask, "What kind of service do you offer?" I would answer them with "any service you need." We would do anything a customer needed in the field of building maintenance. We were always sharply dressed in our company jerseys, hats, jackets and tee shirts. Our uniforms were so nice that people and customers always asked if they could have one to wear. What great advertisement, customers wanting to wear our gear.

Having my own business, built around some very trustworthy employees, afforded me more time to spend with my two teenage daughters, Gretchen and Heidi.

My daughters and my wife were my number one fans along with my sister, Mary Ann, and her family. It was a nice change to spend more time with them doing fun things. It was great to have more time to go to family functions or to just stop by my sister's, mother's or brother's houses and spend quality time with them. I was now doing things with my daughters. Anything they wanted to do from fishing, shopping or going to the beach. Being with them was a great time in my life. I learned to become a spectator. I was watching my daughters grow up.

You would be surprised what you could learn if you just listened and observed. They really let me into their lives. When you're a teacher and coach, it's your job to improve the student or players you're working with. Those years that I was out of teaching and coaching, I was being coached and taught by my daughters. They definitely improved many talents. I needed help in patience, the ability to be a good listener and not to overreact, the need to give things time before making an important decision.

Every so often they would ask me, "Dad, why don't you help out in town coaching? It would be fun to be an official cheerleader for a team you coached."

FIFTEEN

The following season a football assistant position and the head wrestling job opened in my hometown of Middlesex, NJ. It was a temporary position teaching elementary physical education in the neighborhood school. I enjoyed this position immensely. Everyone wanted to do good from the morning bus line to classroom education, cafeteria, and play period. All everyone wanted to do was give the students a good learning environment. What a place. I loved it, plus I could do both teach and coach, and still have time to run my business.

A group of parents in town approached me regarding these coaching openings and asked me if I would be interested. I felt this might be tough being an assistant, especially to a coach who was an assistant coach when I played high school football there twenty years prior. But the real positive was I knew all of the kids and their parents and more importantly they knew Don Somma.

My businesses were doing very well and I had more free time than I needed because I was organized, so I decided to have some fun and took both jobs. I analyzed the situation and recognized what was broken. The kids needed to make a greater commitment, become a little more disciplined and most importantly they had to "listen" to someone. Why do kids listen? Is it fear? Is it respect? Is it loyalty, or is it they like the person who is telling them what to do? I truly feel it's a little bit of all of the above.

My reputation in town was what it was. I was from Middlesex where we were all a little cocky. They knew my door was always open and I could always be counted on to help kids. During my coaching career, even though I was very occupied with my own responsibilities, I helped about a half dozen kids from town obtain football scholarships and about the same amount worked for my company in the summers, so I knew the heartbeat of the community.

My assignment on the football staff was going to be the offensive coordinator. The first thing I did was tweak the playbook, especially the passing game. I knew what they did offensively because years back I gave the head coach all my notes and books on the Veer offense, which was the offense Middlesex ran. The biggest problem was getting the players to listen and do exactly what they were told to do without question.

Coach Murphy, the head coach, took the responsibilities of the kicking game. We had a great defensive coordinator and I was going to be the coach in the press box along with the offensive coordinator assignment. My game day responsibility was to call the offensive plays and assist the defensive coordinator with our opponents' offensive alignments. On paper it looked great.

Things went well initially and we started out 5-0. On offense we were scoring a lot of points and looked very sharp running the 'Veer' along with our three-step passing game. We kept a lot of pressure on the defense in a predominantly running league with our offensive concept.

The people in town were excited again and it was great to see the stands packed. Each game it became more difficult to deal with Coach Murphy regarding play-calling and on the night of our sixth game, everything came to a head at Roselle Park.

I went to the away games with one of the seniors who would drive me in my Jeep. He was the epitome of a high school guard, loyal and an overachiever. It was a lot of fun and both of us laugh when reminiscing about those pre-game Jeep rides. Nothing like having an Italian chauffeur dressed in a football uniform. He was a tough high school guard, a position that is seventy-five percent desire and twenty-five percent ability. I was blessed to coach some great ones who fell into this category. All of them were about 5'9" to 5'10", weighed between 170 to 185 pounds, but had hearts of a lion and a commitment that was unquestionable.

Well, we were playing a team who was also undefeated with a great tradition. Right from the beginning of the game things were very different.

Up until this point, I would call the play down to Murph and he would use our wide receiver rotation to send the play in. Early on in the season, there was no questioning of my decision of what play to call. But the last couple of games, he started to question me about what play to call. It started to become a problem.

Right from our first offensive series that night, some of the plays I called down were not the same plays being sent in and we were having difficulty moving the ball for the first time all year. By the second quarter, he was changing two out of the three plays I was calling and our offense was out of sync for the first time all year including our preseason.

We went in half-time and coach and I had a verbal confrontation prior to going into the locker room. We decided if he wasn't going to listen to me then there was no need for me to be there. I stopped communicating with him halfway through the third quarter when he wasn't listening to me at all. We lost our first game that night and I felt we as a staff let our kids down because of egos.

The next day at our coaches meeting, which I had a tough time going to, the head coach and I agreed that he was "in charge," but I made my point regarding why change something that was working so well and he agreed. We then ran off three straight wins and won our sectional state championship. We were now state champions with an 8-1 record, the best in a long time.

We still had one more game to play, our Thanksgiving game against Manville, a team who had fallen upon some tough times and was a big underdog. Over the last three games things were almost back to normal, but things would never be the same between the head coach and me. This being the last game of the season the problem would end because we both realized this love affair would definitely be over.

Things were like the Roselle Park game when he wasn't listening to my play calling right from the start and got worse by the end of the second quarter. Half time was nuts! There was a lot of finger pointing and arguing between players, and coach was really getting into some of the players' faces. I initially had the frame of mind to stay out of it and let things unfold and accept the outcome.

As things really became negative it was time to become an "actor." I interrupted all the commotion with a talk about unity. I used the example, if I punched the chalk board with an opened fist, I would not be able to break it since I would probably break a finger or two, but if I made a fist depicting working together—at that point I paused and with all the stored up energy I had, I punched the chalkboard and put my fist through it. Point made!

We went out and things were a little different. Coach and I communicated a little better and we scored on our first possession. The next two possessions, we didn't communicate as well and found ourselves trailing with about nine minutes to go.

It was time to do something drastic. I broke the voice control on the head set. So now there was a reason we could not communicate. I yelled down from the press boxes, asking coach if I should come down on the field. He had no choice except to move me down. The defense did a great job and held them. After the punt on the fourth down, we got the ball back deep in our own territory. I took over the situation because I believed in my coaching ability and we had an exciting eighty plus yard drive and went up with less than a minute remaining on the clock. We held them and it was over. It was over in more than one way.

At the end of the game after the locker room cleared out, Coach and I had some respectful parting words. Sometimes decisions have to be made with emotions put aside. I meant no disrespect and I truly felt my decision to do what I did was good for the team. The players and the people in town would always remember the championship year of '84-'85.

It was now wrestling season. It was one of my most enjoyable coaching stints. We based our whole concept on no one was going to outwork us or have more fun doing it "our way." We decided it was important and we set our goal on winning another state championship.

We were having a great season, but there was a problem and the students' safety was in question. By the time we were arriving home from our away matches, it was late at night and the school was locked up. This was 1984-85. Cell phones weren't around yet. The athletes and cheerleaders didn't have access to the school or phones to call their parents. I wrote three letters prior to the season and two after our first away meet explaining that the school being locked was a problem, explaining that our athletes and cheerleaders needed to get into the school for a lot of reasons upon returning from matches. I asked them if they could have a custodian meet us to let us in, or give me a key and I would be responsible for letting them into the building and then be sure it was locked when the last student was picked up by their parents.

After two home victories, it was now time for our second away match and I was told someone would be there to allow us into the building. Upon our arrival back home close to midnight after a big victory again, we found the school locked. Again "action" had to take place. Knowing that the police would come, I yanked open a door to the gym so our students would have access. As they were using the phone, one of my friends who was on the police force arrived. I told him what I did and he said everything was fine, just be sure to lock up. I said, "No, everything isn't fine. Please file a report." He started laughing because he knew why I wanted a report filed. I wanted the principal and superintendent to know what I did and why I did it. I also wanted the police report in the local paper so people in town would understand our dilemma.

The following day, I was called down to the assistant superintendent's office and he told me a letter of reprimand was going into my file. I thanked him for it. From that point on, every time we came home from away matches there was a custodian waiting for us.

At the end of a state championship wrestling season, I helped the Booster club raise money to get the kids who played football and wrestled state championship rings and jackets. Not only did we get them for these participants, but also the managers, trainers, and cheerleaders, which my two girls were a part of. It was fun. We did what some people thought was impossible. Together we raised all the money needed to pay for everything with some money left over which we donated to the all-sports Booster club.

Mission accomplished. By now my business was really growing so I decided not to coach for a while. I also wanted to spend more time with my daughters before they left for college.

SIXTEEN

I enjoyed my time away from education, but something was missing. My business was doing well and again I had too much free time. Both my daughters were now in college so I definitely needed a hobby. I came to the decision that what I enjoyed most was helping young men and women get the most from their high school experience. There was nothing like Friday night lights and the excitement of a packed gym watching a great wrestling match to help the morale of a high school and fill the void I was missing.

I started interviewing for a coaching and teaching job again and a local job was very appealing to me. After two interviews I was offered a job at Manville High School. My responsibilities were to be K-12 physical education coordinator and head football coach. I was also told that if and when a wrestling assistant position opened I would be able to apply for it.

Manville's football program had fallen on some bad times. Participation numbers were at an all time low and it was hard to remember the last winning season. But there was a time in the 60's and early 70's that it was a feared program, so there was a solid tradition to build on.

What really bothered me was the stigma given to the students and athletes. Participation was very low in most extracurricular activities and there wasn't a strong interest in doing their best in the classroom. The youth of Manville were doing other things with their free time besides enjoying the experience of positive high school years in and out of school.

I evaluated the facilities and most of them needed to be upgraded. The game field needed a facelift.

A positive was the amount of space we had for practice. There was more than enough for both soccer programs for boys and girls. The area allocated for football was large enough that we had two football fields. There was a so-called weight room that was very antiquated. You could not find an outdoor basketball hoop in town anywhere that was completely in order. The youth programs were in place, but the kids were losing interest by the end of their middle school years. The physical education budget needed to be increased in order to give the students a positive experience. There were some very good teachers in the physical education department, but we definitely needed to improve their teaching areas. The overall appearance of the exterior of the high school complex needed some tender love and attention. I accepted the position in mid-July, so I had about five weeks to get things ready for our first practice.

First things first. I followed my procedure—why change something that worked so well so many times before. After a four-year rest, I was exploding with energy again. I met with everyone in town who wanted to spend time with me. I needed a lot of help if we were going to make a difference.

What was exciting was there were truly more people who wanted our concepts to be successful. The administrative support I felt initially was solid. The assistant principal and athletic director were good people who really cared about the town of Manville. I made up my mind I would not worry about making decisions that might cause waves. I had already left tenure four times in my career, so I wasn't going to worry about pleasing everyone. The students of Manville were definitely going to be my priority.

A retired CEO of a major world-wide corporation told me later on in life, "If you're going to make decisions and solve agreed upon problems, don't worry too much about social graces and after success is achieved remain humble." It was interesting that this was my method fifteen years prior to hearing his concept on achieving goals and solving problems along the way.

It was important that I got the message across to the rising seniors about the commitment I was willing to make. After meeting with them as a group, I felt very good about their decision to get on board. This was a group of seniors who never felt the enjoyment of a successful season in their high school career to date.

With their help, we recruited every possible athlete out of a class size of thirty-five males. These senior candidates, eleven in all, helped me recruit about thirty percent of the total male population in grades 9-11. About fifty percent of our candidates had experience of some kind with organized football. The other half did not. Five years later, this number of thirty percent of the male population increased to sixty-five percent. My last year in Manville, we had approximately sixty-five student athletes involved in our program, along with another thirty plus involved in the band, cross country and soccer. So we had approximately ninety percent of our males doing something very positive in the fall season. Along with this involvement, the academics and behavior of our students really improved. It was a beautiful thing watching the school, parents, and community collectively working toward a common goal again.

Pre-season went well and we won our opener. Now it was time to play a non-league contest against a state championship program. Immaculata High School, which was located in the town that bordered Manville, was one of the best parochial high schools in the state. They dressed 100 players for a varsity game. That was more male students than we had in our school.

They scheduled Manville like a big Division I school would schedule a small Division IAA school. It was an early season tune-up game, a game that would help them get ready for their league play.

Placement of personnel and using their talents is key on any level and we used our athletes' talents that day to the maximum. We designed a game plan that allowed our athletes to perform based on their abilities. Our concept was simple again. We attacked our opponents' schemes, not their personnel. We emphasized to our players if they did exactly as they were coached, we would shock Immaculata before they had time to adjust.

We played a flawless first half and we were up by two scores going into the locker room. The hitting was ferocious. Just before half time, our fullback was tattooed and sat out the last series prior to the end of the second quarter.

In the locker room halftime, two of my starters said they were scared. Wow, this was a first in twenty plus years of coaching. Thank God I acted instead of reacting to that statement. What I did was move these two players to defense solely after I asked them if they would rather hit someone than be hit. Both of them smiled and agreed with my decision.

The second half was a real battle. We scored one more time and they finally scored. What a victory!

My athletic director said he couldn't wait to go to church the next day and see all the Immaculata fans. He said he was going to go to all three masses so he could see them all. After that victory, they decided not to schedule Manville the following year and never have since.

After football season, we really concentrated on upgrading our facilities. We raised money to do this with every kind of fundraiser you could think of along with donations from some great people and companies who were friends of mine and the program.

We prioritized and came up with a list of things we wanted to improve upon.

The overall outside appearance of the high school was the first area we wanted to improve. We planted flowers everywhere. We planted over five hundred plants and put the freshman class in charge of watering them and keeping them looking good. This was a project that this class did all four years they were students at Manville. We also installed a new welcome sign in front of the high school. This sign was made by a group of students in our shop classes and beautifully painted by our art class. The next thing we worked on was making sure all the basketball goals throughout the town were repaired. Finally they all had backboards, goals and nets.

A good friend, who owned a landscaping company, built an outdoor sand volleyball court for us with sand left over from a highway job. He also was the person who donated the flowers and plants that we planted around the school each year.

During the late sixties and seventies there was a very active quarterback club in town, but during the early and mid-eighties as the decline in the program took hold, so did the involvement of this program drop off. But with the help of Ned Panfile, who was the coach during the glory days, the club had a major renaissance.

It was amazing what this group did for these kids. They single-handedly raised enough money to have state of the art lights installed on our game field and practice area and equipped a new weight room that we built at no cost to the board of education. We took fund raising to the next level. During my tenure at Manville, this wonderful group raised over $100,000 along with another $35,000 in donations of labor and material from some very generous local contractors.

I really believe a class in fundraising should be a part of a teacher's curriculum while they are in college especially coaches and band directors. Talking about band directors—it is so important that the football coach has a positive relationship with everyone involved with game day. The best trumpeter also was a football player. One of the greatest sports photos that I had was a picture of Doug in his football uniform marching with the band during a half-time performance. Yes, one of our captains and a two-way starter marched with the band and performed a solo during halftime instead of coming into the locker room during halftime and he did this in his football uniform. It was quite a sight, but it was Manville. We did things differently. All the extracurricular people worked so well together for the good of the overall atmosphere of the school.

Our triangle of coach, parent and school with the student in the middle was in place and our student athletes' behavior and academic progress were definitely on the upswing. It became important to achieve good grades. This attitude was developed by all involved. It definitely was "we, not I."

As a coach, teacher and parent, I felt it was important to understand and listen to the music your players, students, and children were listening to. I am not knocking all heavy metal, but some of the messages being sent in the late eighties and early nineties I truly didn't agree with and more importantly it did not do much for their rhythm. To combat this I hired an aerobics instructor who was tough, beautiful and in great shape. Twice a week during our pre-season, she would teach classes to our athletes. Not only did we improve our physical well-being, but our number of participants improved greatly. Along with our new weight room and improved outdoor facilities which were used by the total population of the school, exercise and play became vogue.

After our third season things were going well, but with sunshine rain must come. People, especially teachers and coaches, feel what they are doing is important and want their programs to be successful AS WELL . . . I am from the school that believes a program or programs that improve should not affect others in a negative way.

Well, I went head to head with the middle school principal who developed a temporary rainforest. She used the middle school gymnasium. It was only supposed to be used for a short time, but it wound up closing the gym down for physical education classes for over a month for no logical reason. I was against extending the usage of the gymnasium and voiced my opinion.

I was overruled by her and my high school principal. This was a bad time to be at odds with two of my superiors and I was told by these two new first year principals that they were going to be against my achieving tenure. I let it be known that if that was how they felt I would stand on my own merits.

A month earlier, I was asked to interview for the vacant head football position at Paterson Eastside. The principal at Paterson was the famous Joe Clark. Hollywood was in the process of making the movie, "Lean on Me," based on how he improved the attitude and discipline in this tough inner-city school and more importantly how he got the students excited about passing the state exam. It was a very interesting experience and the process went well and I was offered the position. I told them I needed some time to make a decision.

I talked to my athletic director at Manville soon afterward and he sadly said I should consider accepting the position because he was told by the principal that she and her middle school buddy weren't going to recommend me for tenure to the superintendent. Once the parents and community of Manville found out what was going on, the next board meeting was moved to the auditorium because of the turnout of support for me. I hadn't given Paterson a decision yet, but had to do so by the end of the week.

I was never so humbled in my life. The support that the community gave me was overwhelming. That night another first took place. I was told by the state teachers' union representative that this was the first time that he could remember that a principal's decision regarding granting or not granting tenure was overruled. Now how do you leave that kind of support? I decided to decline the great offer from Paterson and I stayed at Manville two more years. Our football program played .500 ball and we finally beat the last team on our schedule that we never beat, not to mention we beat our rival Middlesex five Thanksgivings in a row. Also, years four and five I was involved with the wrestling program and was a part of winning two sectional state wrestling championships as an assistant coach.

The last two years at Manville were enjoyable although the principal of the high school vetoed my department chair position something she could do because this wasn't a tenured position. By doing this she felt she was taking some of my decision making responsibilities away from me.

She decided to make the shop teacher, with no physical education background, the chairperson of physical education. Go figure. So back into the classroom I went and I truly loved it. How tough could teaching two weight room classes and two aerobic classes be? I was also assigned a middle school physical education class. I enjoyed the student contact especially all the different ages of the students. I was enjoying teaching. Well, those last two years went by quickly and it was the winter of my fifth year.

Joe Clark, the famous principal of Paterson Eastside, again contacted me after two unsuccessful football seasons at the school to see if I would interview for the football position there. I was honored that he would call me back after turning the position down two years prior. I now felt I knew the interviewing team even better especially after watching the great movie "Lean on Me" twice. He told me if we could win a state championship he felt a sequel to the first movie would be a definite. They came up with a financial and professional package that was unbelievable. But something didn't feel right and I put them off while I interviewed at another inner city school, Irvington High School. Irvington High School made Paterson Eastside look like a nursery school. But a new principal, assistant superintendent and board were starting to turn things around.

On paper, Irvington had some interesting programs. A preschool tutoring program was in place along with academic and social monitoring programs. I was told that academic and social behavior criteria was also being followed which governed athletic participation.

Now leaving Manville would be a very tough decision. I loved this community and will never forget the parental and community support I received there. Those five years I spent there will always be remembered. I recall telling the parents and players my first year at Manville that we will know when the program is back. It would be when if you didn't arrive at the home games an hour before kickoff you wouldn't get a seat. Well, by the fourth year not only were the seats filled, but it was two deep around the fence. The 50/50 raffle at the home games gave our booster club a major financial boost, not to mention the increase in sales of our logo sweatshirts, hats and other athletic wear.

Goodbyes are tough, so like a thief in the night I got permission to leave immediately and started the Irvington job in the middle of the school year. So I left along with my memories—some of my favorite being:

- Using the flower trick again, we beat Middlesex the first year to break a losing streak to them and won the next four games against them.
- When we finally beat New Providence High School for the first time, we received a standing ovation from their fans.
- When we repaid Ridge High School, a school that was three times our size for running the score up on us.

The following year after that terrible defeat, we beat them going away and for the first time in my career we ran up the score on an opponent.

And one of the funniest things I did while preparing for a game was we were having an offensive drill practicing getting the play called, and lining up as quickly as possible, taking the first step of the play, then sprinting back to the huddle and doing it again. The reason I liked this drill so much was because you emphasize listening to the play and snap count—get out of the huddle, line up properly, getting up as a team together and taking the proper first step. After breaking down so much film, I realized how important these things were to increase the chances of the success of the play no matter what level of football being played.

As the story goes, as we were doing this drill, one of the many pretty girls at Manville walked by the fence near our practice area. I was talking to my players and all eyes in the huddle weren't on me, but were on this young lady as she walked by. While they weren't paying attention, I stopped talking and walked away. Before they knew something was up, I was thirty yards away. I just kept walking. Finally the quarterback ran down to me and asked me what was up. I told him I had it! If you don't want to pay attention, I might as well go home. Well, that night I got half a dozen phone calls that I didn't accept. Then finally a car load of seniors came to my door who I told my wife to send home, after telling them I'd see them at the field in the morning for pre-game preparation. They came, and boy were they ready to play that day. We won by five touchdowns and could have scored three more if we wanted to.

And lastly what I feel was our greatest achievement over our five year tenure was that every senior who wanted to play football at the next level got the opportunity with five of them receiving full football scholarships.

Finally, thank God, it was good to know I would also feel welcomed among the townspeople of Manville, a wonderful community.

SEVENTEEN

The night of the final interview for the Irvington job, the other finalist and I were asked to come to the question and answer period with the interviewing team. It was exciting. I was the last interview. With my experience interviewing and selling jobs, being humble, I realized it was my job if I wanted it. I did a lot of soul searching. Could I help? What could I do and what was I willing to do? I felt comfortable with the interviewing team . . . the principal was a good man, an honest man, plus he was of Italian heritage. There was an assistant superintendent who I felt very comfortable with. Finally, the board member whose job it was to pick and support the choice as the board representative was there.

I met a committee of three seniors prior to this meeting over some good food at a local restaurant. All three got a football scholarship with two of those young men earning their college diploma.

I saw and felt a strong "want," like when I was a little kid I would smell the gravy and really couldn't wait for my first meatball.

Well, I decided, when it was my turn, these were the things I needed.

a. You've got to get paid to support your family. Get a good contract.
b. Opportunity only comes once. Let them know what it was going to take.
c. Same goal—everyone on the same page.
d. Support

During the interview, I convinced all involved we could pull it off, we could win; win in the classroom and on the field.

After the interview, I was walking out to my car when I saw the other candidate standing talking to the police. I walked over to see what was wrong when I was told that the other coach had his car stolen. They left my old truck alone. I often wondered if that had anything to do with them offering me the job instead of him.

Inner-city public education was and still is how you are starting to imagine it. Money was not the reason for schools failing in the inner-city. Failure to give the students and faculty a clean, safe, well-lit facility was the main cause along with allowing a strong leader to do his or her job without interference.

The facilities at Irvington, especially in the physical education and athletic area, were the worst I ever was involved with. We had one field to both practice and play on. The town started to build another field adjacent to the school, but there was so much vandalism and contractor problems that it was ruined before it was ever finished. The pool that they attempted to build turned into a dumpster for the neighborhood.

The physical education and team locker rooms were in terrible shape. The showers and toilets were constantly vandalized and it was almost impossible to find one in working order.

I remember once walking into the physical education locker room and found a student using the unlit shower area as a toilet. I asked him why he was doing this and his answer was that none of the toilets worked and he also felt safer in the shower area.

Who do you blame, the student, the new department chairperson or the new principal? No, the fault should be blamed on the person in charge which at the end of the day was the superintendent. I had very little contact with him and when I went to him I made that point. The superintendent wasn't involved in my hiring and neither one of us knew each other that well. When I explained to him about the deplorable conditions in the physical education area, he looked me square in the face and said, "Your problem, Mr. Somma, is you think you're our hope."

I answered him saying, "I'm the only hope you've got."

Irvington was one of the last districts in New Jersey where the mayor appointed the board of education members. The board representative for athletics who hired me was replaced shortly after I started and the assistant superintendent left the district about the same time. The principal, who was a great man to work for, was replaced shortly after the end of the school year for political reasons. So the three people who were involved with me during the interview and hiring process were no longer there. I was on my own. From the time of my hiring to the end of that first school year, a lot of positives took place during the first four months thanks to the opportunity they gave me, but now they were gone. These were the people who put together my teaching responsibilities along with setting the goals we wanted to accomplish and how we were going to do it.

My position was a non-classroom teaching load. During the school day, my responsibility was to work with the student/athletes making sure they went to class and to get as many as I could to become eligible as soon as possible. Progress was being made. This was a work load that was kept in place until the people who were responsible for putting it together were no longer involved with the high school. Then it was a constant battle with their replacements to maintain my responsibilities. It was just another thing to overcome.

When I arrived at Irvington at the beginning of the third marking period, the first thing I did was meet with the rising seniors and their guidance counselors. I was shocked when I saw their grade point averages. Only three out of the fifteen rising senior candidates had better than a C average and, if I enforced a new district policy that stated all student athletes' grade point averages had to be a 2.0 or better, I wouldn't have enough players to field a team. This policy was in place for almost a year, but was not being enforced.

There was an athletic study and tutorial program both before and after school. On paper it was a very well designed program. Four teachers were receiving a stipend to be involved with the program and the athletic director gave me the responsibility to oversee the program and make sure it was done right and keep good attendance records of both the faculty and the athletes. Initially I had more trouble getting the tutors there on time with a positive attitude.

After discussing this problem with my superiors and putting it in writing, I was told to keep attendance on both the student athletes and faculty. It took a couple of weeks to get everyone, both student and teacher there on time and doing things for a purpose, with a purpose. I could see I was again rustling feathers making peers accountable. But, so what? We had to. It was too important. It was our job to give these kids a chance to learn.

Approximately eighty percent of the football candidates didn't have a 2.0 and had to attend. I said if candidates didn't attend I would notify their parents immediately. So with parental assistance, we got our players to school on time and helped them start and end their day in a learning atmosphere. During the school day, I would literally walk students to class and constantly check on them to make sure they were behaving. Sometimes I would sit in on classes to help the teacher with class discipline so they would be able to teach and the students had an opportunity to finally learn in a safe environment.

One of the rising seniors really grasped the attitude of learning and pushing himself in all areas. Not to just single him out, but every senior who wanted to go to college and play football got the opportunity to do so with half of them taking advantage of that opportunity, obtaining diplomas, and also doing a great job playing football. That special student's name was Raheem Morris, who became the head coach of the Tampa Bay Buccaneers in January of 2009. Talk about reaching a goal and utilizing your capabilities!

I was a month into the Irvington job and was dealing with every possible cause for the condition the program was in. I would pray for patience every morning on my drive to work knowing that it was a difficult thing to pray for because you don't know you have patience until you're tested. Being tested was putting it mildly. I was staying strong by not wasting energy by being over-emotional. I learned early on that coaching is like a ferris wheel ride. There are stops along the way. Sometimes you're on top rocking and enjoying the ride knowing it's not going to last, and soon you'll be at the bottom getting off.

My father was in the hospital for one of his routine check-ups and I talked to my mother in the evening and everything seemed to be fine. So as I was driving to work, my mind was pretty clear and I was mentally getting ready for the problems that were awaiting me. My first meeting that morning was with the athletic director to discuss the morning study hall. Some things were being achieved and we were starting to have some semblance of academic order.

Thanks to the guidance office, we now had class schedules for all of the potential football candidates. We contacted the parent or parents along with their teachers and everybody understood what we were trying to achieve. Did everybody agree with the procedure? No, but things had to change at this point if we were going to follow a school policy which looked great on paper. We wouldn't have enough players to field either a varsity or a junior varsity team, but we were making progress.

After the meeting, I was ready for my daily routine—covering study hall—checking the morning breakfast program—and then going to all the homerooms to see who was present and on time. If a player wasn't in homeroom, I would immediately call his home or parent at their job to see why he wasn't at school on time.

Contact, contact, contact, communication was extremely important. I wanted everyone to understand the effort that was needed to achieve our academic goals. It was now first period and the clock was ticking. This day I was working with the rising seniors. I would literally walk them to class and in some situations, sit in class to help the learning environment so the teacher could and would teach. Just close your eyes and visualize the worst classroom behavior possible. It was that bad. But, with a group effort, the classroom behavior improved. The word got around fast that I wouldn't tolerate this unbelievable unruly behavior. We would talk about paying attention, taking notes and, most important, letting the teacher know we wanted to learn and achieve good grades.

After first period, before I went back to my office to go over the daily progress reports, I felt a need to call my sister to see how my father was doing. When my sister answered the phone she was very upset and said that for no logical reason Dad had taken a turn for the worse and I should do my best to get there ASAP. At that moment nothing else was on my mind except finding out how I was going to get to my father as quickly as I could. As soon as I hung up the phone I went to the assistant superintendent and told him I had to leave immediately. He was a good man and he told me, "Don't waste any time, do what you have to do."

I went to my office, called in two rising senior leaders and told them I would be back when I had some control over the situation. I immediately drove to Newark airport. As it worked out, within an hour I was on a flight to Raleigh where my parents had lived for the last two years. My brother and sister moved there first for professional reasons and my parents decided to move there shortly afterwards.

During the flight, I was thinking what day it was. It was the Feast of St. Joseph. The feast day of a humble man who took care of problems in a quiet humble way. He had to be firm but fair. We know he taught his son how to be hard working and always do things like a craftsman. He was a good father, a good husband and a protector of his family—traits my father always showed.

By the time I got to the hospital, my father was in a peaceful sleep—a sleep that he never woke from. For the next two hours while I sat with him, all I thought about was what a fair man he was and what he taught me about family, always giving never taking.

When my father finally passed, there was such a feeling of peace in the room. Just him and I—my father was getting his final reward, one that he was always committed to and worked hard to achieve. Catholics believe and are taught that he who dies on St. Joseph's Feast Day will be rewarded with a peaceful death and at the moment I knew everything was okay.

The process of grieving or dealing with any emotional moment I believed should be controlled as quickly as possible and utilized. On my trip back to New Jersey with my wife and family I was thinking about so many things. But one thing just kept on jumping out. I kept on remembering that my father was tough but fair and he didn't need to tell me he loved me every day. I knew he did. He was a good man that I loved and respected very much.

He always said to me, "Take care of the seniors and spend time with them." He used to love the stories about taking the players to five-star restaurants, fishing trips and trips to the Jersey shore. I made up my mind then to give the rising seniors a great year in my father's name . . . to share time with them away from football to really let them understand they had to set goals and work to achieve them, but sometimes you need a little real good honest-to-God hard love.

Reality set in quickly. Six-thirty a. m. the next day I arrived at my office and found my door kicked in and my office ransacked. Just another challenge. I sure felt my father's presence—don't get upset—re-gather yourself and take this new situation straight on. I went out to my truck, got my tools, fixed the door, cleaned up my office and now I was ready for the next ride on the ferris wheel.

When I took the position, they told me I would be allowed to bring in as many good teacher/coaches as I thought would be able to work in the environment at Irvington. I brought in my two sons-in-law who captained and played at South Carolina and a third past captain from USC who played some professional football and was hired to be a hall monitor. One of my sons-in-law worked in the physical education department as a full time teacher. Jay, my other son-in-law, after one week in the classroom, decided he would only coach there and not teach because of the unruly environment. Tough to believe how bad it was. Irvington High School's population was about ninety percent black and the black on black fighting was terrible.

To round off my varsity staff I hired three past student athletes who played for me when I coached at Elizabeth. During the day, they worked for the state penal systems so they understood the environment. When they got off work they came and did a great job coaching and mentoring.

From my first day on the job, and what a day it was, I arrived at school by 6:00 a.m. Well that day I realized why the teachers with the most seniority got parking places closest to the entrance of the high school.

Since I was the new kid on the block, my parking space was in the rear of the back parking lot. After a long first day, it was about eight-thirty p.m. when I left the building. When I arrived at my car, it was broken into through the side window. My radio and stereo were stolen along with some personal items. I drove home that cold winter night with no music and a broken window which allowed the cold winter night to come in. Talk about not feeling sorry for yourself. It was time to deal with driving south on the Jersey Parkway on a snowy night with no music.

The Irvington football schedule was extremely tough and I was again back in one of the toughest if not the toughest conferences in the state. It was one of the reasons I took the job. I loved the competition especially playing against Union, a team that had a national reputation. I followed the same script, developed a great staff and came up with a coaching philosophy designed to attack and defend Unions' schemes, a coaching philosophy which I knew and understood from my days at Elizabeth. It would be an honor to coach against Lou Rettino again, a Hall of Fame coach and, more importantly, a great man.

Over the next six months I worked six days a week recruiting as many athletes as I could and made sure they were going to be eligible.

Since the 2.0 rule was in place, I made sure we followed it to the letter.

Every Saturday morning during the next two semesters, I would meet with our football candidates who weren't involved in winter or spring sports and we would teach them our playbook. Before summer, the major portion of our coaching philosophy was in place. Prior to us leaving for camp in Pennsylvania in late August, everything was in order. Our camp experience was something to behold. It was a lot of fun and very rewarding watching these inner-city student athletes enjoy the surroundings of the outdoors.

At the beginning of school, the new principal added to my responsibilities. She told me that I would be involved with discipline during the school day. I told her that I wanted Emanuel Weaver, the man I hired to coach our defensive line, to work with me in the halls. Emanuel was 6'5", 275 lbs., and was tough as hell, and he had a lot more street smarts than I did. Weaver was special and I trusted him.

He was a great guy to go down an alley with. My favorite Weaver story was how he controlled a major fight in the cafeteria by just being him. There I was one lunch period trying to break up a potentially dangerous situation when I saw this giant of a man running across table tops. Without missing a step he picked up a sixteen foot long table and pinned the combatives, all six of them, against the wall. It was quite a sight to behold.

Another area of concern was the physical education area which included the gymnasium and our game field, which also served as our outside physical education teaching station. And, I use that word, teaching station, with tongue in cheek.

During a class period, over 250 plus students would be assigned to physical education. On an average day, half of them would not participate in class by either not changing for class or not attending. It was a paste and stick lesson plan. It always looked good on paper but in reality it was a roll-the-ball-out attitude with little or no supervision. The ability to institute the program was lacking and who really cared.

Remember how important the closest parking space mentality was? But I was of the attitude of give the student a chance, a chance to learn and thank God some took advantage of the opportunity and somehow they learned.

The teachers in the physical education area were a close knit fraternity that I definitely did not fit into. For whatever reason, they felt the school was hopeless along with making things better hopeless. I had a major confrontation with the physical education faculty early on.

Picture 250 plus students, milling around the gym—some playing pick-up basketball, some trying to play volleyball. Most of the students were socializing in groups. All of a sudden, a student throws a very powerful firecracker into a group of students injuring two of them. When this occurred, my son-in-law ran out of the gym chasing the student who threw the firecracker. Not one of the other teachers followed him out to help. When I found out about this I was very upset to say the least. First, I gave my son-in-law a lecture about not trusting anyone to cover your back. Then, I lost my temper with the teachers who had a chance to help and follow my son-in-law down the alley, but chose not to do so. I really drew a line in the sand that day with a certain group of teachers. I let them know how I felt about them not covering a fellow teacher's back.

From that day forward, the teachers in that area really made things difficult. I had to make sure the students who participated in football changed for class and did their best to do something positive in a very negative situation. There definitely wasn't any special program for the athletes during their physical education class or any help from this area for our quest to turn around Irvington's football program.

One night a week, and on Saturday mornings as part of our off season program, I hired a good friend of mine who was a personal trainer. He held three black belts in various martial arts disciplines and used aerobics as a method of conditioning his students. He was a young-looking forty year old, well-educated black man who related well with teenagers. To prove a point, I asked him to come one morning a week during May and June prior to the official opening of school. I opened his session to any student who wanted to participate in this class at 7:00 a.m. We filled the gym with over 150 from general population including our athletes and we had over 200 participate including some faculty members. What a sight to behold, students listening, wanting to learn, and a teacher teaching. One who was on a mission to do his job teaching disciplined movement, togetherness, ability to take command, conditioning, having fun—positive experience. The majority of the students were the same kids who wouldn't participate in their "normal" physical education classes. Point made—offer a good program with a purpose and students would participate.

Before I knew it, August arrived and we had approximately thirty-five varsity candidates who were eligible. I felt very confident. I had a small army ready to become a team.

We convinced a couple of basketball players who previously didn't play football and a handful of students who I met in the halls to get involved in our program. Remember, this was a formula I used in all the programs I coached in. You must get every potential athlete in the school out for football if you hope to turn things around.

Upon returning from a week-long football camp in Pennsylvania, school was starting. Right from the start, the problems took place between fights, fires, and false alarms. We were averaging emptying the building three times a week. The new principal asked me to use our football players as hall monitors to help in assisting getting the students in and out of the building. She trusted our abilities. We would place our seniors and junior players throughout the building to help facilitate the students in and out of the building. Initially, I agreed and things worked, but because it was happening so often I became worried about their safety and I stopped using our athletes. Truthfully, it wasn't our job.

That fall my responsibility during the school day was challenged. The new physical education department head wanted me to teach two classes a day. I said, "No way" and I told the principal no way would I be involved with the attitude in the physical education area and if she backed the department chair I would challenge her decision. That's when she assigned me to help out with school discipline.

Along with Emanuel, we would be called to unruly situations. It was like being a bouncer in the local night club my senior year in college. Taking knives and other weapons away from students, putting out fires and breaking up fights became a daily experience. If you enjoyed excitement and physical altercations, it was a fun job. That fall, as discipline deteriorated daily, it was difficult to keep our kids focused, but somehow we stuck together and stayed focused on the task at hand. Stay eligible and be ready game day.

We opened the season with a road victory over a conference opponent. We played a very good game and won easily. Finally, it was Union week. Union, the year past, was state champion and finished Number One in the State Poll. They were now ranked Number Two in the state and had a national high ranking in USA Today. We were underdogs and the papers that week didn't give us much of a chance to win.

We did our best all week in school to keep our kids focused on the game. We had a very good week of practice and it was finally Friday and we were on our way to play Union at Union—Friday night lights. It was an overflow crowd. The state paper made it a real big deal with headlines reading, "Somma's Next Challenge."

It was not me who was challenged, but it was a challenge to my players who were challenged just to get to school, make it through a school day and then return home safely. It was even a bigger test for them to learn something in an environment that definitely wasn't conducive to learning. That's what the headlines should have been about. The goal of doing something positive with their lives and getting away from this environment, and then, if they chose to do so, return and make a difference. One thing was sure that Friday night. We were ready to play a great game from warmups to the opening kickoff to the final whistle. We were prepared.

I knew in the fourth quarter we were going to pull it off. We were going to win, not just look good. The Union players were arguing among themselves and saying to each other that they were acting and playing like the Irvington of old while we were playing like Union teams that had national rankings and feared reputation. It was a proud moment.

We played flawless football and were almost penalty free throughout the game. Our execution and play selection in all three aspects of the game was something to watch. It was almost like we had our scouts inside their huddles and knew their schemes and play selections before the snap. No videotaping of their sidelines took place. No congressional hearing was needed. As the game ended, our players and coaches were greeted at midfield by our opponents and were shown the respect that we gained during the game.

Coach Rettino, a Hall of Fame coach who was my old rival from my Elizabeth days, hugged me and at that moment in time I really felt a mutual love and respect. Since his death two years later, a day doesn't go by that I don't say a prayer in his memory. He sure was someone special, someone I wish I knew better as a friend and not only as a rival.

The good feelings and sportsmanship ended quickly. There was a lot of commotion going on in the stands and the parking lot. When I heard gun shots, my mood changed quickly from joy to very worried and concerned. Talk about a major mood swing. My wife and two daughters were there and I became very nervous about their safety. My two sons-in-law ran to make sure they were safe, and I and my staff made sure that our players and cheerleaders got on our bus safely.

It wasn't a good time in the mid-nineties. There was a lot of violence in the inner cities. Thank God no one associated with our program was hurt physically, but I was emotionally upset and angry. It was hard for me to understand why these kids were so angry and violent toward each other. But as I stated earlier, always understand the message in the music. The gangster rap concept was definitely not sending out positive messages. Even though the beat and rhythm was great, the youth listening to it was receiving mixed messages.

The black on black violence was constant. May it be youth who were from different countries fighting or kids from one town fighting with kids from another town, whatever, it was physical violence like you could only realize if you saw it. To see another human being shoot someone over the way he looked at his girlfriend or a student hit another student in the head with a baseball bat because he was from another country than he, was difficult to understand.

The Monday morning after the Union game, we found ourselves ranked in the state's top twenty teams for the first time since who knows when. We kept our players on target the best we could in such a difficult surrounding. Sometimes I didn't know what was more dangerous, them getting to school, being in school, or getting home.

One thing for sure after the school day was over, our practice field was a special place for two hours a day. All that mattered was the task at hand, prepare for victory. Nothing else mattered. Practice was our escape.

Rules, reasons, method—all enforced for the common goal. Winning on Friday night, Saturday or whatever the game day was.

If I had to guess why, I would have to say it is truly want—you must truly want "it". Bottom Line.

We remained in the top twenty throughout the season until we lost our last game and didn't qualify for the state championship.

We finished our season with a 6-2-1 record, and all eight of our seniors who wanted to continue playing football in college got the opportunity to do so and received full football scholarships. Four out of the eight who went on and attended college took advantage of this opportunity and graduated. Given an opportunity, some people take advantage of their chance. Why some more than others? After the recruiting process was over his senior year, I remember Raheem telling me that I looked and acted old and very tired for the first time since he knew me. It was the truth. I was tired of fighting the system. I was physically challenged from two tough altercations. Tired for the first time. The behavior in the school was hard for me to accept and I was starting to understand why so many of the faculty felt the way they did. Strong leadership was needed and surely there was none. A lot of programs, but no leadership. There definitely wasn't a boss, someone who had a plan, and more importantly the ability to make sure his or her ideas and methods were followed.

EIGHTEEN

It was early fall of my second football season at Irvington. A lot of things were different this go round. My two sons-in-law decided not to come back, along with one of my past players from Elizabeth. But they were replaced by some good assistants, one of them being Kirk Hamrah who was with me in Elizabeth. He always made a great commitment in everything he did. With the right support Kirk could make a difference in an environment such as Irvington.

School discipline was definitely on the decline for a lot of reasons. With a very young fragile team coming back, I knew the battles were going to be difficult.

The administration had some ties to some entertainers who were big on the pop music charts. Two groups were asked to come to the school and put on a mini-concert during the school day in the gymnasium for overall school spirit.

The first group came out and the leader made a speech about how the gangs should not fight with each other but should join forces. His delivery of the message was definitely reverse discrimination. Before you knew it, there weren't many faculty members nor any administrators to be found. By the end of the set I was one of a handful. The final song caused quite an uncomfortable atmosphere. The lead singer would shout, "Who is the toughest M _ _ _ _ _ F _ _ _ _ _ in the house?" after each verse. The student groups, who were sitting in their areas, jumped up and chanted, "We Are!" You had to see the climate. It was nuts!

By the last go round, he noticed me because I was standing right next to the stage. Not knowing who I was, he started goofing on me and my racial background. When the final go round about who was the toughest M _ _ _ _ _ F _ _ _ _ _ in the house was about to be sung, it was time for me to get involved and do my best to control a very potentially violent situation.

The majority of students respected me and almost all the students knew me, so when I went to the microphone and took control before a bad situation turned into an even worse situation, I was well accepted and at the moment I was the toughest guy in the house. I raised my hand and let the students know who was in control. I dismissed one section of the gym at a time. Thank God I was able to get everyone out of the gymnasium safely, including the last group standing—our football team.

The negative energy that had built during the concert spilled out into the parking lot a half hour later. There were some fights in the parking lot along with well over $10,000 of damage to cars which were still parked in that area.

That afternoon, I exploded in the principal's office for the fourth time in the past six months. I really let my emotions go and let everyone understand how I felt. That was my Italian heritage taking over.

There were two situations prior to this that forced me to go into the principal's office to vent; one being a major riot that took place at a college fair for scholar athletes throughout New Jersey. They scheduled schools in to the fair at various times of the day. Around mid-day, they scheduled the majority of the inner-city schools at the same time. Having these students from the inner city together proved to be a poor decision. A major fight broke out that took three police forces from neighboring towns along with the state police to control. At least half a dozen students and chaperones received major injuries. There were countless minor bumps and bruises to other participants. I was able to get the eighteen students who I was responsible for out of the exhibition center, onto the bus, and home safely. In doing so I received an injury to my neck that forced me to seek medical attention. When I returned to the school, I broke down in the principal's office, explaining to her about what happened and told her how this constant violence and lack of discipline was becoming a major concern.

These kinds of situations maybe received a paragraph or two in the state paper, but in today's world of 24/7 news it would have gotten national attention. In my opinion, the state's largest newspaper avoided those politically sensitive topics. I really feel they didn't want to expose the inability of offering a safe and quality education in some of New Jersey's inner-city schools. It was definitely a political time bomb.

The principal stated it was over and said be thankful for getting our students home safely. She almost brushed it off as no big deal. But it was. This anger was hard to comprehend. But, if you understood and listened to the music of the times you felt it and I really believe it added to the problem.

Shortly after the end of my first football season, a situation occurred that caused me to age and took away my energy and desire to fight. Two intruders came into the building and took two sets of fifteen pound dumbbells. I saw one of them run out of the weight room and I chased after him knowing that he was probably going to use them as weapons, plus they were ours. When I finally caught the one I saw, I put him up against the wall in the alley adjacent to the school and parking lot. All I told him was I wanted the dumbbells back. Not knowing that there was another person involved, I started walking away. The second intruder, who was hiding behind a car, hit me in the head with the dumbbell he took. Somehow I stayed on my feet. I looked him straight in the face. I was almost out. He ran and after I got my senses back, I chased them for about fifteen blocks. Finally I accepted the fact that they got away, but at least I was able to retrieve both sets of dumbbells.

I walked back to my office a little dazed and I filled out the paper work explaining what had happened. While I was writing up the report, one of the school's tough guys who didn't play sports but definitely knew the streets came into my office. He said he heard what happened. He told me I was a "fair" guy who treated everyone the same and he respected me for that. He told me he knew the two punks who did this and he knew which one hit me because he was already bragging about what he did. He asked me if I wanted him to "cap" the punk who hit me. I said, "Please don't do that, but you could bring him to the office the next day instead." He asked if I wanted both of them. I said, "No, the only one I want is the punk who sucker punched me with the dumbbell."

Well, you had to see the scene in the principal's office the next day. There I was in the office with the intruder, his mother, the principal and the woman who was in charge of security. Before you knew it, they were listening to his side of the story. He was telling them he was feeling threatened by me and my reputation.

Because initially I didn't have a witness and didn't know that someone saw what happened, the school wouldn't press charges. If I wanted charges brought against this person I had to do it myself. When that punk left the office with his mother, I went off on both administrators and told them how I felt and why our school was like it was. Thank God by the end of the school day after the story got out, a faculty member finally found time and the nerve to write up a report saying he'd witnessed what happened and collaborated my version.

Now the school was able to press charges and a court date was set. This happened so often at Irvington where a board of education employee was assaulted that it was no big deal in the press. It was like an everyday occurrence. There was no 24/7 news then so it was kept rather quiet.

Two weeks went by and it was a week before the trial date. As I was walking out to my car, I saw the kid who sucker punched me. He stared me down and made threatening remarks. I said to him, "This time you'd better kill me because if you take one more step towards me it will be your last." I never had such rage in my heart as I did at that moment. Always in my professional life I was able to control myself in threatening situations without violence, but this time I felt no control and I knew he sensed that at this moment I was ready to be violent.

I walked back into the building, told the principal what happened. Again, same question. Were there witnesses? I said, "No." Her answer was the same. It was up to me to press charges on my own. I went to the police station and did so.

After the juvenile court trial, the youth was found guilty and received a nine-month sentence and two years probation for assault and battery, not assault with a deadly weapon with intent. The public defender kept pushing the issue that his client felt threatened by my reputation even though I never saw this person in my life prior to the altercation. The judge bought in.

The environment was difficult and, yes, I was tired. My coaching suffered the worst. I was missing two to three days a week from the pain. My coaching and ability to be the leader I needed to be was falling apart. With this very young team, outside influences were tearing them down and we weren't achieving in the classroom or on the field.

There were so many situations which affected the overall environment that you started to find sick humor in them to tolerate them. A couple examples which really stayed with me still bring a smile.

One of those was when I called time out on the field so I could take care of a bad situation in the stands. It was during the homecoming game. Dressed in the stands with their king and queen crowns on were the principal and superintendent. We were the Knights, the Blue Knights and they were in "charge" of it all. You had to look at the coaches from the other team. They knew me and knew Irvington. It had to be done or the game would have ended in one big fight. With the help of security, I had two students who were instigating another group of students removed from the stands. All this was going on while the administrators who looked like clowns rather than the school mascot, looked on.

I fought off the pain as long as I could and finally went to the school doctor. His therapy was pain medication and muscle relaxers. After about six months of this I was unable to function. I went to him and told him I was about to do something I would be sorry for if he didn't allow me to go see a doctor of my own choice. He finally gave in and wrote me a prescription to go see an orthopedic doctor who I knew. I went the next day. I was sent for an MRI and within days I was on the operating table having a crushed disc removed from my neck.

After the operation in February, 1994, I never returned to Irvington. It took me ten years to recuperate and have a semi-normal physical and mental life without pain medication. I have learned that physical pain is like any other pain. You must learn to accept it. You learn that it is a test and thank God it has helped me to become a better person.

To this day it is troubling that certain goals I set for the Irvington program with the group of people who initially hired me were not achieved. The thought of winning a state championship and helping improve the overall atmosphere was achievable, but only with the support of the administration which changed abruptly. That senior player was right when he said I looked tired and lost my fight.

I resigned after the season and was operated on shortly afterwards. A disc was removed from my neck from the two altercations I received within six months. The football coaches stayed loyal to each other and did a great job the following season.

For the next couple of years most of my time was spent rehabbing the physical conditions caused by my injuries.

NINETEEN

Following the 1997 football season, Robert Toresco, who left education after being the head coach at Elizabeth, got in contact with me about the condition of the football program at Hunterdon Central High School. Bob, who worked with me at both North Hunterdon and Elizabeth, was now a developer in Hunterdon County. For fun he volunteered his time to the community and was in charge of their Pop Warner program.

As with everything Bob did, the Pop Warner program was flourishing. The team that Bob coached had just won the national championship in Florida at Disney World. Bob asked if I would hang around the varsity program and give him my opinion of what was missing. The practice field was about five minutes from my house. At the time I was still rehabbing and couldn't get around too well so this was a good reason for me to get out of the house. I told Bob I would do so and I would get back to him.

The Hunterdon varsity program had fallen on some hard times and the W's were few and far between. The coach was being blamed and a great majority of people who were interested in the program felt a coaching change was necessary.

I started observing the program during the summer of 1998. After a few weeks, I noticed how much flack the head coach was getting from the players, assistant coaches, parents and booster club members. No matter what the head coach would do, someone always had a better idea or method of making things better. The athletic director was not someone who I would want covering my back in a tenuous situation. He was more concerned with his own job security than helping the head coach keep his.

The football practice and game facilities were in poor shape for a Group IV high school, especially one that bragged so much about being a blue ribbon school district. I lived in this district and it disturbed me how poor the facilities were especially because of how much tax I was paying. In New Jersey the schools are financed mostly from local land taxes and Readington Township taxes were among the highest in the state.

The negative comments about the program and lack of staff, administrative and community support, definitely were affecting how the players felt about the leadership of the football program.

After a few weeks of observing the program from the outside, I finally sat down with the head coach. Jim Meert was a good guy who really needed someone who he could count on. Initially, Jim wanted me to become a paid member of his staff. I declined the offer and told him I would rather volunteer my services to the program and use the position as a paid assistant to bring in some young blood which was definitely needed.

I discussed my observations with Jim and told him exactly how I felt about the conditions of the program. I told him it was obvious that the commitment level and support from administration, coaching staff, parents and players wasn't there.

After the fourth week of the season, I again sat down with Jim and said I could fix the situation. But things would have to be done in such a way that all decisions would go through me.

By doing this I took the pressure off of Jim and onto me. We started to do everything with a purpose. We developed a method of practice organization, game planning and game day decisions. As always some people initially weren't happy but progress was visible from day one.

We taught the staff how to meet and make collective decisions with the understanding that at the end, the final decision of how to get things done was going to be mine. Jim let it be known that was my job. Now all methods and plans were coming from the top. Once we agreed there was no deviating from the plan, we finally had follow-through and things started to get better. After starting the season 0-4 we finished 4-5. Now people bought in. Jim made a major decision and allowed me to spearhead our quest to turn this thing around. I really liked the volunteer concept. It enabled me to do things and not be worried about job security.

The winter and spring went quickly and the time to get ready for the 1999 season was approaching fast. This was a great outlet for me. I was using twenty-five years of experience to fix something I had the confidence and ability to do. But it had to be my way, not that I wanted to be in charge, but I had to be. We developed a coaching concept that things were going to be a certain way, no other way, but this certain way.

Now when the kids went home and were asked about how things were being done, no one would question the concept because they knew we had an organized plan, a plan that was proven and was going to be followed to the letter. It's not that I always enjoyed being the boss, but I realized I had the ability to be one. More importantly I wasn't afraid to make a decision. Normally it was a decision that I gave a lot of thought to. Yes, there were times that a quick decision needed to be made but because of my acting ability I always gave it a few seconds before pulling the trigger.

During all the interviews I went on, people would ask what kind of offense, defense or kicking game I planned on implementing. I would always give the same pat answer. I would say, "I don't know. I have to get to know the athletes, understand the league and develop a staff."

Well, we had seven months to do this. It was time to convince the staff as a whole that things were going to be done in a very organized way, a script that was used many times and a record of success. I used all my years of experience to develop a coaching concept that would utilize our talent and aggressive attitude. Jim made it known that all decisions were to go through me and it was my job to convince everyone involved that the methods agreed upon were the right choices. What a great job. Jim took care of the administrative work and I put together an offensive and defensive playbook. The coaching of the kicking game was also handled by Jim.

There were some problems initially, but most importantly the kids bought in. They liked the new structure—everything definitely had a purpose and method.

Finally the athletic director was helping, but from my experiences I knew if a problem arose we couldn't count on his support. He was the type who would definitely sway and would take the politically correct stand if needed. The athletic director's position wasn't a tenured position so he was very interested in being politically correct.

We were having some problems getting the weight room opened and monitored. That's where Bob Toresco and his beautiful wife, Debbie, came into play. Bob volunteered his house and basement weight room. It was like Rocky training in the neighborhood gym. The environment was great. The rising sophomores, juniors and seniors trained at Bob's house, and the freshmen used the school's facilities. Bob put into place a great speed and strength program, and Debbie always had a pot of meatballs and spaghetti upstairs if anyone was hungry. Talk about building camaraderie—it was a beautiful thing to watch. Things were definitely being done a certain way, our way. Everyone was on the same page.

The summer flew by. We had a very productive pre-season. At the time I still was having difficulty with my ability to deal with my physical problems—of not being able to be on my feet and get around due to the injury that I sustained at Irvington.

When the word got out that I was having problems, the building and grounds crew offered to let me use a golf cart that they used during the day which allowed me to move around the practice field.

We were so structured, everything we did had a purpose—everything had a reason—everything led to our goal of being state champs. Our concept was to be relentless in our approach to the game. Each individual had an assignment. We made them believe in self, then teammate. It was really amazing how beautifully they played. We executed our game plans almost flawlessly, winning all twelve games on our way to the state championship. We got to showcase the fruits of our labor on the big stage at the Meadowlands, winning both the state semi-final and final games in front of 20,000 plus spectators. This team was extremely competitive. Our turnover ratio was +31. This is an amazing stat. The turnover ratio is one of the few statistics that as a coach I felt was worth keeping and usually led to the direct result of who won the game.

This championship run was the result of twenty-eight years of coaching experience along with thirty years of the experience of running my own business and being allowed by a real good friend and fellow coach to do what was best for the program.

During my coaching tenures, I would not have been given the opportunity to be the head coach if something wasn't broken. All the programs had something wrong with them. If they didn't, I would not have been given the chance to figure out what was wrong and then fix it. The template was always the same—first you must be given the opportunity to be in charge and somehow get the people who you are leading allow you to make choices and follow through on these choices.

A head coach or person in charge must be able to answer to himself. He must be able to make decisions and not be afraid of the repercussions these decisions will lead to as long as he feels that they will help the task of achieving the goal at hand.

In all the coaching situations we were involved in, the goal was to give the players the opportunity to be a part of a positive winning environment both on the field and off. The definition of a winning program was always defined by both the person, or persons, who hired me and myself. Collectively we would set the goal and then I would come up with a plan on how we would achieve this goal.

If everyone was on the same page the journey was a beautiful thing to watch and be a part of.

There are a lot of quotes tied into football and coaching. The one "Football is like war" is used quite a bit. I never liked it, or believed it. Finally at sixty-one years old, I heard a better analogy. Don Drobny, who is in charge of the Marine Scholarship program in South Carolina, where I now reside, compared war to football, but a more serious version. This comparison put things into proper order. Since my involvement in this wonderful program of helping children of our Marines achieve scholarships to attend college, I've been given the opportunity to in a very small way, be a part of one of the greatest "teams" I've ever been associated with, the United States Marines. IN GOD WE TRUST.

The methods I've used as a coach and businessman to solve problems and reach goals has definitely been perfected by the world's greatest fighting force, The United States Marine Corps.

After watching these young men and women train at Parris Island on a few occasions, I am so thankful to be an American and when I go to sleep each night I thank God for these young warriors who keep our country and freedoms safe. What a team. They are Champions in every sense of the word. All they do is do what they were trained to do with confidence in their teammates.

Having the privilege of watching what the marines do best, that is to "build men" or women, I reinforced my objectives of being a good grandpop and coach for all my grandchildren. I really enjoy helping them be better at what they choose to do. But, isn't that what a coach-teacher-parent or boss should do—help them at what they are doing or what they might do for the first time? It's quite a responsibility to "tell" someone what to do, especially when they believe what you say.

TWENTY

I was taught in my college freshman English class that the final chapter of a story has to bring the message to a "Finale."

This past April, 2011, my daughter, Gretchen, her husband, David, and their children moved to Bluffton, South Carolina, into a house about ten miles from where I live.

My oldest grandson, Dillon, was going to get the opportunity to play organized football for the first time. The middle school he would be attending had a seventh and eighth grade football team. Prior to their relocating, we checked out the school district and everyone was pleased.

The new head varsity coach of one season, the fall of 2010, really turned things around quickly on the football field. Their record that year was 12-2 and was the first winning season since the high school opened nine years ago. From observation the overall discipline and participation of all involved was very good.

During the spring practice, which took place in May of 2011, it was evident that the program could really become special in all aspects . . . school, its football team, and community involvement.

After watching from the other side of the fence, I was considering the possibility of getting involved with the program. I met with the head coach and we discussed my desire to volunteer my services.

One of his goals for the 2011 season was to run all four sub-varsity programs the exact same way the varsity program ran their program.

After meeting with Coach, he asked if I could help institute his coaching and organizational philosophies with the participants of the seventh and eighth grade football program. Any decision I made had my family's blessings.

I made up my mind to contribute my time. Over the years I have realized how important time is. Yes, time is a gift and you'd better manage it properly. What you do with it is your gift back.

August, 2011, came quickly and the season was about to start. All of the challenges were similar to my past experiences. No one person was more important than anyone else. We had to define behavior and responsibility and in some way get all involved to realize what it took and what must be done to field a team. We had to build. In order to build, as always, we had to get everybody on board; teachers, student participants, coaches, support staff . . . all pulling in the same direction. All participants had to be on the practice field cleared to play, dressed properly and yes, on time. Once we had everyone involved there, then we had to keep them there. We had to maintain their interest, keep them socially and academically eligible and during this time we had to also teach them the skills needed to play.

Each participant had to be identified and placed in a position to utilize his talents. We had to get all involved to prepare for victory by competing against self in everything they did throughout the school day, on the practice field, and finally the game field.

Early on during the process I was pulling on my experiences to see if I could recall any memory that would help me with our purpose. One specific memory kept on coming to mind. Everyone is important, but there is in every program that one participant that is the glue that keeps everything in order. The water boy/equipment manager/roll taker—because, yes, he was the one who learned all the participants names first and finally was the all important holder of the keys! Everything he did, he did to the best of his ability always giving maximum effort. It was very obvious that he wanted to be there. It was also clear that everyone in the program counted on him never questioning his ability to do the many jobs with which he was entrusted.

Here I was at this point in my life, an old man, learning from a young kid.

He was beautiful to watch and I realized what a humble position he held but without his efforts we would never become a team. It was decided by the head coach that we would use his example in hopes that all of the other participants would understand the effort needed.

It took some time, but by the fifth game of the middle school's season, things clicked. The team realized by the example of the water boy, what was expected and they were giving the effort needed.

I worked my way into a position on the football staff that I really enjoyed. I became the water boy's assistant. From this position I was able to watch a group of young teenagers led by a group of coaches who worked together for the first time to become a team. They learned to work toward the common goal of giving their best on and off the field, truly understanding what it meant to prepare and practice for victory. Yes, I was in South Carolina. But my memories were in Jersey, remembering all I had learned as a young boy watching my grandfathers. This time I was watching my own grandson and his teammates learning how to be team members and enjoying the great game of high school football . . . I had come full circle.